8-25-'69

Melanie,

Happy (late!) mmnday!

αγαπη

Dick

BLUE
DENIM
AND
LACE

BY

DR. JACK HYLES

Pastor
First Baptist Church
Hammond, Indiana

HYLES-ANDERSON PUBLISHERS
HAMMOND, INDIANA

PRINTED IN THE UNITED STATES OF AMERICA
BY
E. J. DANIELS, PUBLISHERS
P. O. Box 3428, Orlando, Fla. 32802

TABLE OF CONTENTS

FOREWORD

One of my staff members said to me one time that he wished that he could feel as deeply as I feel. He asked me for the secret. I made it clear that one of the main secrets is practicing the art of meditation. In these days of busy cities, busy activities, and busy schedules, how neglected is this spiritual grace. In the first Psalm we are reminded that meditation is necessary for prosperity. Paul reminds us in Philippians 4:8 that we are to think on things that are true, honest, just, pure, lovely, and of good report. In I Timothy 4:15 Paul admonishes young Timothy to meditate on what God had done for him. When Joshua assumed the leadership of Israel, he was reminded in Joshua 1:8 to meditate. In Genesis 24:63 we find that Isaac was a man of meditation. In Psalm 63:6 David reminds us that he meditated through the night.

I have found it wise to have a set time and set place for meditation. It is something that should be done on purpose. *Meditation is love's nourishment.* No one can properly love unless his mind dwells on the love and on the loved.

If one is to develop the depth of soul that he should have, he must of necessity spend time in meditation.

In order to have proper gratitude, one must meditate upon the things that God and others have done for him.

If improvement comes in our lives, it comes only after soul-searching meditation which leads us to realize our weaknesses, imperfections, frailties, and need for improvement.

Meditation enables us to escape the traps that Satan sets for us in order to capture our minds. Drive down the average highway and look at the signs that seek your mind's attention. Add to this the television, the radio, the thousands of people with whom you come in contact regularly, and the million other things in life and you will find the mind has little chance to be alone. Hence, it is wise for a person to set a time and a place for meditation. This has been my policy through the years. In the following chapters you will find some of these meditations. Some have been during the night watches; some have been while flying 30,000 feet in the air, but all have come through meditation. May God bless you as we together "think upon these things."

Chapter One

WHEN TIME IS NO LONGER

". . .that there should be time no longer." (Revelation 10:6)

Perhaps one of the hardest things to define is time. *I have often thought of time as being a yardstick with which to measure deterioration.* Could that be the reason there is no time with God, and there will be no time in eternity? Nothing will ever deteriorate there. There will be no depreciation; hence, there will be no need for the measuring stick — time.

The older I get the more I realize that perhaps the greatest gift that I could give you is my time. Actually, the only gift that I can give is my time. If I give you money, I give you the time it took me to earn that money. If I give you a gift, I give you the time it took me to earn the money with which I bought the gift. Perhaps, then, it is true that time is the only thing that I can really give to you. Time is probably the greatest gift for several reasons:

1. *When I give you my time, I am giving you my life, for time is life.* If one takes the life of another, actually he takes only time from him. Murder is simply taking from a person the amount of time that he would have lived anyway. So in a real sense, when I give to you my time, I am giving to you my life, for time is life.

How much more could I honor you than to give you my time? How much more could you honor me than to give me your time? My time with you is an investment. Your time with me is an investment. Let us care for each other's investment wisely.

2. *If I spend some time with you, I am giving you a gift that can be given only to YOU!* The moment that I give to you I will never have again. Once it is given, it can never be given to another. Such a realization should cause us to appreciate moments spent with friends, for a moment given to me by a friend is not only his giving to me of his life, but

9

also something which he can give to no other person and which can never be given again.

3. *For you to give me a moment, or for me to give you a moment, is to exchange the only moment that we actually know we have.* We are only promised the present. When we share the present with each other, we are giving to each other the only moment that we have for sure. There may never be another.

4. *The giving of a moment to a friend is a greater gift than Heaven can give.* If I spend a moment with you in Heaven, it will not be subtracted from time, for there is no time there. In Heaven I will not be giving you my life, for life is eternal there. Here is an earthly gift that I may give you that I cannot give you in Heaven, for to spend a moment there is not a sacrifice. May I then never take lightly the time you give to me, and may you never take lightly the time I give to you.

5. *Time is a gift God cannot give.* God gives us many wonderful gifts. This is one thing that God cannot give you. God has no time. He does not give up any of His life to fellowship with you. To be sure, He gave His life on the cross to save you; but since God will never die, the time He gives to you and the moments you share with Him do not subtract anything from His life. In other words, He loses no life to fellowship with you. However, when I fellowship with you, I lose my life. When you fellowship with me, you are giving of your life. Here is a gift we can share that even God cannot give.

6. *For me to give to you a moment is an honor that God cannot give you.* When we share a moment alone, we take that moment from everyone else and give it to each other. God, however, is omnipresent. For Him to fellowship with you does not mean that He must forfeit fellowship with all others. Hence, when you give me a few moments, I must pause to realize that you are honoring me above all of the people of the earth for that moment.

Therefore, to give you my time is the greatest gift that I can give. Since it can be given only to you and only to one person at a time and can never be given again, please accept the moment that I give as my supreme gift, and as an expression of my love to you and my interest in you.

Recently someone asked me this question: "Why do you make everything seem so sacred? It seems that you make the least little event such a sacred occasion."

I have given you my reasons. Every event of life uses up a little more of the most precious commodity that I have on earth — my life. The event may seem trivial and the occasion may seem small, but the price that I am paying is the greatest price that I have to pay. Hence, I do not measure an occasion by its greatness or bigness, but by the price I pay for it — even my life.

Chapter Two

THE ADVANTAGE OF THE FRIEND RELATIONSHIP

Life is a series of human relationships. It is very important that we develop each to its fullest. No one need magnify the importance of the parent-child relationship, the husband-wife relationship, the brother-sister relationship, etc. There is, however, a need to magnify the importance of the friend relationship. Many would never class it in importance with the aforementioned. I think that it should be. Let us observe some advantages in the friend relationship.

1. *It is one of the few relationships that we choose.* We do not choose our mother, our father, our brother, our sister, our son, our daughter. God chooses them for us. Because He does, they are sacred relationships. There are a few relationships, however, that should be akin to those mentioned above. These are made sacred because they are chosen by us. One such relation is that of a friend. If I am your friend, I chose to be your friend. If you are my friend, you chose to be my friend. What an honor we have given to each other. Of all the people in the world we have given our friendship one to the other. How sacred such a relationship!

2. *It can be a completely unselfish relationship.* The child needs the parent. In usual cases, in later years the parent needs the child. The husband needs the wife, and the wife needs the husband. In each of these relationships there is, however holy, a righteous selfishness involved. When I chose to be your friend, however, I chose to give and not to receive. I chose to help and not to be helped. I chose to love and not to be loved. I chose to care for you and not to be cared for by you. In being your friend I ask nothing. I am willing to give everything, which means that the object of such friendship may rest comfortably in an unselfish relationship.

3. *Friendship is one of the few relationships that never changes.* The child grows up and leaves home. The parent grows old and passes away. Brothers and sisters move away from home. At first the child needs the parent; later the parent needs the child. Even in marriage the needs change

12

with the passing of the years. In friendship it need not be so. Many parents will admit that about the time they learn how to be parents, the children are grown. The same is true with m a n y relationships in   life, but the friend relationship is one of the few, if not the only one, where one can spend years becoming an expert and still have time to use what he has learned, for the relationship may remain the same.

4. *The friend relationship is one that can be for life.* The age difference in the parent-child relationship often causes it to be a brief one, but because friends normally are in the same age bracket, it is a relationship that lasts longer than do most relationships.

5. *The friend relationship is one that needs not the acceptance of another.* To become a husband means that another must accept the proposal. To become a wife means that there must be a proposal by another. True friendship is not, however, based upon this. I can be your friend, even if you are not my friend. In other words, friendship need not be reciprocated. This means if I am your friend, I have chosen you from a wide field of possibilites. I did not choose you because you accepted, for I became your friend before you accepted. In some cases, I am your friend even if you never accept, but what an honor it is to have a friend!

6. *One need never give up one friend for another.* In some relationships of life there can be only one. In the friendship relationship the one relationship need not be traded if another is acquired. This relationship is never lost to another. You may be my friend and someone else's friend. When I become a friend to another, I may still be your friend.

7. *The friend relationship is one that can be completely spiritual.* Most of life's relationships are based upon physical needs. To be sure, there are spiritual needs also. In any relationship of life the spiritual should be uppermost. I can become your friend, however, without there being one physical need for you to supply. Our souls may be knit together, and our relationship need not be based upon the satisfying of physical appetites.

8. *A friend may be chosen at any time of life.* Parents come at birth; children come to us in young adulthood;

brothers and sisters come to us during childhood. People at a certain age are unable to have children, but a friend may be chosen at eight or eighty, nine or ninety, ten or one hundred, sixteen or sixty.

Friendship is a high and lofty relationship. Few ever know its depth. Most never know a friend, and certainly, most never are a friend.

Hence, the great relationships of life are husband-wife, mother-daughter, father-son, brother-sister, and . . . friend. *Happy is the man who has a friend. Happier is the man who is a friend. Happiest is the man who has a friend and is a friend. Oh, how happy I am.!*

Chapter Three

THE IMPORTANCE OF LITTLE THINGS

Sometime notice in your Bible the many little things that were of great significance: the little gift of the widow, the water pots in which Jesus performed His first miracle, Shamgar's ox goad, Moses' rod, etc.

There is no doubt but that one of the great differences between success and failure is the importance placed on little things. There has to be a reason why men of equal talent do not have equal success, and oftentimes, men of less talent have greater success than many-talented ones.

Often a successful person will be called a perfectionist. He will even be criticized because of his overemphasis on seemingly "trivial matters." *It might be wise, however, for less successful people to examine the methods of those who are successful, and in so doing, not criticize the differences but rather pattern after them.* The differences between people is composed of their differences. Our differences cause our difference. Hence, it might be wise for one to emulate rather than criticize a so-called perfectionist.

1. *The only way to excel is to do the little things.* Everyone does the big things. They are the things that challenge each of us. Consequently, the difference between us must be our attention toward little things. I have noticed very carefully successful people from every walk of life. The so-called trivials mean something to them. The nonessentials seem to be essentials. Everything seems to be big. They have found that "little drops of water and little grains of sand make the mighty ocean and the pleasant land."

2. *The one who cares for little things will be misunderstood by those who care not.* "He is too particular." "He is hard to work for." Similar statements are often made about those who care for details and to whom punctuality, neatness, and thoroughness are important. Hence, when one comes to the place where everything is important and there are no such things as trivials, he is oftentimes misunderstood by his contemporaries.

15

3. *The big is the little.* We have found in our generation that the most powerful force is the splitting of the smallest thing. In the splitting of the atom a succession of explosions can be set off to cause the biggest explosion the world has ever known. This has taught us that the power is not in the big but in the little. The spoil lies to the person who counts the little as big. Oftentimes I have said to my staff, "If a task is worth doing, it is worth doing right. If it is not worth doing well, it is not worth doing." If something needs to be done, it is big. If we have a job to do, it is big. If it is worthy of our attention, it is worthy of our best.

4. *When one does the little thing well, he will automatically do the big thing well.* Someone has said that a preacher should preach to the back row. If the folks on the back row can hear him, certainly he will be understood by those on the front row. When a person does a little job well, he will certainly do a big job well.

Truthfully, who among us is able to discern between the big and the little? So often we come to the conclusion of a task only to find that it was one of the biggest tasks we had ever attempted. None of us can be sure about the size of a task. It should behoove us to do every task well, thereby insuring ourselves of always doing a good job on the big tasks.

5. *The little often becomes the big.* Someone has said, "Be nice to your paperboy; you may try to borrow some money from his bank some day." Someone else has said, "Be kind to the boy who plays in your yard. You may be on trial in his court some day." The safest thing to do is be nice to the little man, do well each little task, preach your best to the little crowds, prepare well for the little jobs, and you will certainly corral the big ones. Remember, the little often becomes the big and the big is often the little. Who is able to judge the difference?

6. *Do not measure a task by its size.* Just do what there is to do. The other day I was parked in front of a big business. I was not surprised when I saw the owner of the business sweeping off the sidewalk. This is the way he got to be a big man. He was a good little man. The way he got to do the big

tasks was by doing the little tasks well. *Greatness is often wrapped in simplicity. A person who is unwilling to do the little will not have the opportunity to do the big.* The person who is not challenged by the little will not be presented the challenge to do the big. *A person who has not done well the little is not prepared or qualified to do the big.* Do not weigh a task. If it is before you, do it and do it well. Even if it is unworthy of you, you, nevertheless, are setting principles by which you will live a life. One who is not diligent in little tasks will not develop the diligence necessary to do the big tasks. *Even if the task is not worthy of you, diligence is; and even if what you do is not big, the way you do it can be big.* Someone will see how you do it and realize that you are qualified to do something bigger. Then too, in doing the small task diligently one is preparing himself with the methods necessary to succeed in a big task.

7. *Always make a check list of little things.* Never trust your memory. You will remember to do the big, but you must remind yourself to do the little. If possible, the little should be done immediately. Fix little things when they break. Most houses become run-down because of the neglect of repairing little things. Many cars lose their value because the little things are not attended to. Make a check list of things to do that are little.

This article is being dictated on a jet plane between Chicago and Seattle, Washington. There I will board another jet for a speaking engagement in Tokyo, Japan. Just a moment ago a little thing was called to my attention. I made a note of it, put the note in my pocket, and will be reminded to do the task and do it well.

8. *In doing the little things one becomes Christlike.* You must remember that Jesus never pastored a large church. He was never a president, governor or mayor. He took time for little children. He told simple stories. He spoke of a flower, a bird, a gardener, a husbandman, a lost coin, and a boy who ran away from home. His Father and our Father takes note of a bird that falls. He clothes the lilies of the field. He is even interested in each hair on our heads. Hence, if we would

be Christlike, we must notice the little things and do them
well.

9. *The degree of unhappiness you have with yourself over
not doing the little things well will determine the amount of
growth you experience.* For one to improve himself he must
realize his inefficiences and weaknesses. Usually the big
things will be accomplished. When one has accomplished the
big things, he may then think that he has arrived. *The growth
he experiences in the future will be determined by how
dissatisfied he is in the present.* Hence, he must find
unhappiness over the failure to do well the little things.

This is true in every field. The baseball player who is in a
hitting slump may find he is jerking his head at the wrong
time. The football player may find that he is not charging
low enough as he blocks. The track star may find that his
failures are caused by holding his arms too far from his body
or standing too erect when he starts to race. In every walk of
life this is the case. Once one has become successful in a field,
his continued improvement is dependent upon his mastering,
not of the big, but of the little. Remember nothing is
unimportant. No task should be taken lightly. Every job is a
big job. Every day is a big day. Every sermon is a big sermon.

When I was in college, I took a course called Pastoral
Theology. It was taught by the president of the college and
was attended by the preacher boys. Each Monday we were
asked to give a report of our weekend activities. On this
particular Monday I was so happy to give my report. You see,
I had just accepted my first pastorate the day before. It was
one hundred miles from our college town. Mrs. Hyles and I
drove there each weekend in our old Dodge. I was the first
preacher asked to give his report on this particular Monday
morning. I stood and said, "Dr. Bruce, I would like to report
that I had a wonderful weekend. I was called as Pastor of a
little church in the country. . ."

Dr. Bruce interrupted me and said, "Sit down, Mr. Hyles."

I could not for the life of me understand why he told me
to sit down. Every other young preacher gave his report, and
there was not another single reprimand given by Dr. Bruce.

Finally when the reports were all given, I raised my hand and asked, "Dr. Bruce, what did I say that was wrong?"

Dr. Bruce replied with an answer I shall never forget, "You said, Mr. Hyles, that you had been called to pastor a l i t t l e . . . c h u r c h . . . M r.   H y l e s,   t h e r e are. . .no. . .little. . .churches!"

I then stood to my feet and said, "Dr. Bruce, I would like to give my report. Yesterday I was called to pastor a big church up in the country with nineteen members at a salary of $7.50 a week."

The class roared with laughter, but I had been taught a lesson I shall never forget. There are no little churches. There are no little preachers. There are no little people. There are no little tasks!

Chapter Four

SACRED THINGS

The Jews had many holy days, special seasons, feasts, etc. Colossians 2:14-17 reminds us that these were nailed to the cross. *"Blotting out the handwriting of ordinances that was against us, which was contrary to us, and took it out of the way, nailing it to His cross; And having spoiled principalities and powers, He made a shew of them openly, triumphing over them in it. Let no man therefore judge you in meat, or in drink, or in respect of an holy day, or of the new moon, or of the sabbath days: Which are a shadow of things to come; but the body is of Christ. (Colossians 2:14-17)*

Paul said in Galatians that he was afraid of the Galatian people who had lapsed back into legalism and the observance of days and seasons lest he had bestowed labor upon them in vain. In his writings the apostle gives much space to the fact that in Christ every day is a holy day and every season a holy season.

Places were also sacred to the Jews. There was the Holy of Holies in the temple as well as other places that became known as sacred. Jesus was talking to the woman at the well when suddenly she interrupted him by suggesting that the Jews worshipped in Jerusalem but the Samaritans worshipped on Mt. Gerizim. He then reminded her, *"But the hour cometh, and now is, when the true worshippers shall worship the Father in spirit and in truth: for the Father seeketh such to worship Him. (John 4:23)* Hence, *there are now no sacred places — only sacred relationships.*

Someone would say, "Pastor, how about the place where you were saved, the spot where you were married, the place you became engaged, etc. — are these sacred places?"

No. The place is not sacred. It is the relationship that is sacred. The place and date are simply made dear because of the sacred relationship. Hence, the Christian should have no sacred places, but many dear places; no sacred days, but many dear days. He should however, have sacred relationships. The spot should be only a reminder, not the object. There are several such spots in my life, such as the place where I was saved, my father's grave, etc. These spots, however, are not sacred spots. These are only places held dear because of relationships and events that are held sacred. Because of this, we should make many of them. With the passing of the years they will be even more dear to us. In order to make such dear places we must find how to do so.

1. *Think now how you will feel later.* One of the tragic *True* things of this depraved human race is that we have to wait until an experience is ended before it has been made dear to us. If the spot will someday be a treasured one, let us make it such now. *Character enables one to appreciate the present as those who have no character will appreciate it in the future.* The chair in which a loved one sits, the pulpit behind which a dear pastor speaks, the organ bench on which an organist sits, the desk of an office worker, and other places will someday become hallowed spots. If this be true, we should appreciate and see them as such now. The things that one is now doing will some day become dear and hallowed things. The rearing of the children, the living of a normal home life, and even youth itself will some day be looked back upon with reverence. Why not look upon the enjoyment as such while it is in progress? As the pastor walks to the pulpit, he should realize that someday this spot will be very dear, so it should be very dear now. When the office worker sits behind his desk, he should realize his privilege while he sits there. It is sad that so many of us have to wait until days are past to really appreciate them.

2. *Remember that the usual will someday become the unusual.* Everything is temporary. Because it is, the usual should be treated as the unusual. That which will someday become the unusual should be treated as the unusual today. A trip to the zoo, a night with the family, the eating of hamburgers at a drive-in sandwich shop, etc. will someday be precious memories. The person with character will make them precious experiences now.

3. *Use the same place.* People who have close ties are happy people. In order to make those close ties there must be familiarity. Some people who love each other meet at the same spot year after year. Others pray for each other at the same time day after day. Others eat at the same restaurant, etc. As an

experience takes place at the same place, or at the same time, it becomes more dear and sacred. Man is a creature of habits. Proper habits can make, not only for treasured memories, but treasured experiences now.

4. *Measure the relationship now.* One of the sad things about us is that we wait until the tree is fallen before we measure it. *Anybody can measure a fallen tree; character measures the tree while it is still standing.* Do not wait until you lose him to know how much you love him. Measure that love now. It isn't death that makes something sacred; it is life. Character makes it sacred now. If you work for a good employer, realize it now! Do not wait until he is gone. If you have a good husband or wife, realize it now. Do not wait until that one is taken.

Look into the future to see the price the treasure will have after it is gone, and place that price upon it now. Do not wait until someday to make sacred the "place where we met," but rather today make sacred the "place where we meet."

5. *Make gifts what they ought to be. A gift is a shrine where the recipient meets the giver and an altar where he thanks God for the giver.* Choose what you wear carefully. A certain tie can be worn as a reminder of the one who gave it. This chapter is being dictated in the Atlanta, Georgia, airport. The cuff links and "tie tac" that I wear are gifts from dear friends. Hence, I am now thinking of them and praying for them. A simple thing such as a cuff link has become a shrine where I meet the giver and an altar where I thank God for the giver. Gifts should be purposely used in order to remind us of those whom we love.

The same is true concerning other objects that remind us of dear ones. Perhaps we shared experiences together in a certain car or we attended the same school. If so, each time we ride in that car or each time we drive by that school, we can be reminded of dear relationships.

6. *A disciplined schedule makes for sacred times.* The person who does the same thing at the same time will find it a precious time. Wise is the person who schedules his time. In so doing, he is building up memories of things that happened at a certain hour so as to make that hour dear and precious in the future. One of the secrets to life is the discipline of time.

This and other things make for close ties and sentimental people. People often say that they are just not affectionate and sentimental. The simple truth may be that they are not disciplined. Proper discipline of time, mind, and life will make for regular activities that may be looked upon in the future as dear ones. With character these can be treasured now.

7. *A route can make sacred places.* There are many such sacred trails. The child who takes the same way to school each morning is making the route a revered one. The man who drives the same way each day to work may do the same thing. Just a few months ago we visited a city where I pastored for seven years. How dear to me was the route between my home and the church because I took the same route each day. It became almost sacred to me. Hence, how happy I was to retrace my steps once again.

8. *Enter into close relationships.* A few years ago as a young man I read a book that had a very vital influence on my life. It was called *Try Giving Yourself Away.* I do not recall the contents of the book; I do recall its title. I decided then and there to give myself away in human relationships. I decided not to be afraid to enter into close relationships. I have never been sorry. Hence, my friends are sacred. My relationships are sacred. I have known intimate ties that I have treasured, do treasure, and will treasure all my life.

No place is sacred in itself. No time is sacred in itself. Hence, if a place or a time becomes sacred, it is so because of relationships and disciplined lives that make it possible. Such discipline and such relationships can make life more meaningful and more worthwhile. They can make every gift a shrine, every bush a burning bush, every spot of ground holy ground, every building a temple, and every day a holy day.

Chapter Five

JONATHAN AND DAVID

One day while conducting Staff Devotions, I was asked by one of the staff members concerning the subject of friendship. The devotion for that day had pertained to the relationship of friends. The question asked was something like this: "Pastor, do you know of any such friends in the Bible?" Immediately my attention was directed toward Jonathan and his relationship to David. This, of course, was one of the most beautiful relationships in all the Bible and is worthy of careful inspection.

1. *"...the soul of Jonathan was knit with the soul of David..." (I Samuel 18:1)* Notice that it does not say that he knitted himself, but that the soul was knit. True friendship is a gift of God, and a person who has a true friend should count him as such. We hear much about "falling in love" in our day. I doubt if anyone can really define such a condition, but there is such a thing in the Bible. God knit the soul of one to the soul of another. The words "made one" could be used in the relationship of Christ and the church as well as in the relationship of the husband and wife. In other words, when God gives one a friend, he knits their souls just as really as Christ was knit to the church and as the husband and wife are knit to each other.

It is worthy of note that Jonathan's soul was knit to David's. David needed a friend. God gave David such a friend. Happy and blessed is the person who knows such knitting of his soul to that of another.

2. *Notice the words in I Samuel 18:1 and 3,* "as own soul." In other words, Jonathan loved David as he loved his own soul. *This could mean "one soul in two bodies," or it could mean "another self."* When God gives such a friendship, He gives a love for the friend that is akin to a love for self. The friend's welfare is my welfare. In other words, we prefer our friends to ourselves. How sacred, how wonderful is such a relationship.

24

3. *Jonathan gave up the kingdom for David. (I Samuel 18:4)* Jonathan was the son of Saul. Saul was the king. No doubt he was the heir apparent to the throne, but his friendship led him to give all to his friend. David's welfare meant more than his own. True love and true friendship knows no bounds of sacrifice, love, and giving. True love gives to be satisfied, but finds dissatisfaction. Again, it gives, but again it wants to give more. Yet again it gives, and again it is unsatisfied. Nothing can satisfy true love but giving all. Such was the case of Jonathan.

4. *This friendship was not necessarily earned.* The word "Jonathan" means "God has given" or "given by God." Apart from salvation itself, God has no more gracious gift than the gift of a true friend. If there is one such person in the world to you, thank God daily for him and do your best to nurture this relationship to its fullest.

5. *The friendship was closer than blood. (I Samuel 19:2)* In Proverbs 18:24 we find that there is a friend that sticketh closer than a brother. In John 15:13 we find that the greatest love is one laying down his life for a friend. True friendship is often closer than blood ties. This is the way God would have it. No doubt many readers will think of some such relationship that they enjoy. How sweet it is when the bonds of Jesus Christ and the bonds of Christian friendship exceed even the ties of blood.

6. *They made a covenant between them to die for each other and to help each other's relatives.* I believe that people should develop friendships so close for which death itself would not be too great a gift. Jonathan proved the sincerity of his heart when he risked his life again and again for his friend David. Each of us would like to have such a friend. It is more important that each of us *become* such a friend. Ask yourself: "Would I die for anyone?" Make a list of people for whom you would die. Once this list is made and you have made a covenant with yourself to offer such friendship, then go to the person or persons involved and tell them of your devotion. Enter into this covenant with them. Of course, do not expect reciprocation. Happy is the person who has love for another deep enough to die for him. It is certainly

important that such relationships be expressed one to another when such friendships develop.

7. *Jonathan was willing to be in the shadows. (I Samuel 23:17)* True friendship is willing to be second. It is willing to exalt the other in place of self. It steps in the shadows and pushes the friend into the limelight. It finds its satisfaction in loving and not in being loved, in helping and not in being helped. It rejoices in the success of a friend.

8. *It seems that Jonathan expressed his friendship to David everytime he saw him.* Again and again he took care to tell David of his love, devotion, and friendship. This is very important in a friend relationship. To be sure, there is an assurance in perfect love. Yet, we are only people, and we need to be assured again and again. There should be an excess of "I love you's" rather than a scarcity of them. How sweet it is when friends express devotion one to the other.

9. *As far as we know, David was the only one to whom Jonathan was such a friend.* One must not assume such deep relationships lightly. *A friend should be as carefully chosen in the will of God as husband and wife.* It is not a lesser relationship. Hence, too many such friends would cheapen the union. Also, because friendship bears with it tremendous obligations, one should not assume more friends than he is capable to fulfill the obligations involved. The word "friend" means far too little in most circles and should certainly carry with it a willingness to give all. This, of course, would narrow considerably the number of friends that any one person could have.

10. *Jonathan gave to David his every desire. (I Samuel 20:4)* True friendship seeks for the needs of its object. As I have said elsewhere in this book, *THE DESIRE OF A FRIEND IS A ROYAL COMMAND!*

11. *Bodily absence does not mean that friends are apart.* Jonathan and David were not together as much as one would think, yet their souls had been knit. There is a fellowship other than physical fellowship. How beautiful it is when the souls of two people are so knit together that they cannot be "separate" from each other.

There are some people in this world for whom I would

die. I have them listed, and each day I pause to thank God
for them by name and to fellowship with them though miles
may separate us. Paul said in Philippians 1:7 that he had the
Philippian people in his heart. In verse 8 he expressed his
longing for them. True friends should have each other in their
hearts and should have such soul fellowship that nothing can
separate them.

12. *It is interesting to note what happened to David after
Jonathan died.* Not long after Jonathan died, David had his
terrible affair with Bathsheba. Then he lost the baby from
this unholy union. A son raped a daughter. One son
murdered another son. The murderer son then rebelled
against his father, fought to take over the kingdom, and was
soon killed in a battle against the forces of his own father.
None of this happened to David while he had his friend.
Could it be that it was Jonathan's friendship that helped keep
David right?

I have known the inspiration that is given by having a
friend. Such relationships can make my preaching better,
inspire me to write more, and even keep my life cleaner and
more dedicated to God. A true friend leads one to
righteousness. A true friend enables his friend to become a
better Christian. Such was the case with Jonathan and such
should be the case with us.

13. *Perhaps David never really understood the depth of
Jonathan's love.* To some, the relationship seems one-sided.
To be sure, David did not have the opportunity to be a friend
to Jonathan that Jonathan had to be a friend to David.
However, the statement in II Samuel 1:26 that Jonathan's
love exceeded that of women seems to me to be a little
shallow. It is doubtful that David ever knew the depth of the
friendship for Jonathan that Jonathan knew for David. We
must remember, however, that David needed a friend more
than Jonathan did. Perhaps it could be that God gave David a
stronger friend because of his need. God's promise is that He
will *"supply all of our needs according to His riches in
glory."* This God did for David and likewise for Jonathan.
There has always been some doubt to me, however, if David
knew the depth of friendship that Jonathan knew. This

should alert each of us to do his best to have sufficient love
to reciprocate the depth of a friend's affection.

14. *David gave to Jonathan after his death.* All
relationships on earth must end for a season, and so did
David and Jonathan's earthly friendship. Jonathan died, but
David's friendship lingered. In II Samuel 9:1 we see that
David did a favor for Jonathan's son in honor of Jonathan
and his life. He brought Mephibosheth, the son of Jonathan,
to the king's palace (though the son was crippled) to live as
one of his own sons in honor of Jonathan. There are those
who think that David should have done something for
Jonathan earlier. Perhaps he waited too late to express his
friendship. Whether or not this is true in this story, it is
nevertheless the case in many lives. We should do now what
we plan to do later for our friends. Let us tell of our love
now! Let us show our appreciation now! Let us sacrifice
now! Let us give now. Let us share now. It is good to give to
one's decendants after his death. It is better to give to them
during his life.

How sweet it is when God miraculously imparts friendship
to two people. There are many close relationships in life such
as parent-child, husband-wife, brother-sister, etc. Along
beside these relationships must go a true friendship – the
kind of friendship that exists between Jonathans and Davids,
the kind of friendship which is a gift from Heaven and which
will last forever.

Chapter Six

DANIEL'S SPIRIT

"Then this Daniel was preferred above the presidents and princes, because an excellent spirit was in him; and the king thought to set him over the whole realm." (Daniel 6:3)

In this verse we find that Daniel had an excellent spirit. There is more to this statement than meets the eye. Perhaps it would be better translated, "the spirit excelled in Daniel." In other words, the spiritual was more important to Daniel than the physical. The unseen was more important than the seen. The intangible was more important than the tangible. The spirit excelled in him.

When Jesus speaks of the end time, He says that one of its characteristics will be that people will be buying and selling, eating and drinking, marrying and giving in marriage. Now there is nothing wrong with buying and selling. There is nothing wrong with eating and drinking, and there is nothing wrong with marrying and giving in marriage, except it is a picture of our day when people excel in the flesh.

Daniel excelled in the spirit. He placed his physical appetites secondary, and the spirit became the chief thing. Here is the reason that Daniel could interpret dreams and obtain spiritual insight which few others did. How tragic it is that even good Christians spend so much time on the seen and so little on the unseen; so much time on the physical and so little on the spiritual; so much time on the tangible and so little on the intangible. *In Daniel, the physical did not possess a spirit, but the spiritual possessed a body.* This is why he could purpose in his heart that he would not sin against God or defile his flesh with the king's meat. This indicates that he gave much thought as to his purpose in life. He found his duties, found the will of God for his life, and built all else around it in a world of materialism and physical attraction.

Let it be said of us that the spirit excels in us as it did in Daniel. Let us major on the spirit. Let us think of and find our purpose in life. Then let us purpose in our hearts that we will do nothing that will steer us from our goal and purpose in life. The only way one could properly do this is to have the spirit excel in him.

Chapter Seven

DO RIGHT

When I was a high school lad, a dear Sunday School teacher named Dr. Rutherford gave me a New Testament. On the inside of it he wrote, *"My son, if sinners entice thee, consent thou not." (Proverbs 1:10)* This became my motto for life.

Billy Sunday used to say, "Do right. Do right if the stars fall, but do right." Such was the case with Daniel. Let us notice several things about Daniel's doing right when he refused to eat the King's meat or drink the King's wine.

1. *It is always right to do right.* Daniel, Shadrach, Meshach, and Abednego would not bow down to wrong. Later Daniel was put in the lion's den, but this decision was made a long time before at the dining room table when he decided that he would always do right. It became a part of his character. It is always a good idea for people just to say, "I will always do right." Let principles make decisions. A person should decide early in life the principles by which he plans to live. These principles can become an IBM machine letting every decision fall where it will according to one's principles. As I look back on my life, I can see several principles that I set as a child and as a young person that have guided me in the making of decisions for a lifetime.

2. *It is always right to do right away from home.* Someone has said that the "real you" comes out away from home. What do you do when away at college? What do you do in the army when temptations come? The real test will come when there is a temptation to do wrong and Mother does not know, Father does not know, Pastor does not know, and friends do not know. Let it always be said that we do right away from home. Many people go places during vacation to which they would never go at home. Many people gamble at Las Vagas who would never gamble anywhere else. How sad.

3. *It is always right to do right regardless of the results.* Always make the decision apart from the results. If right

turns out wrong, it is still right to do right. Right needs no vindication. Right is its own reward. Do not even consider the results when deciding whether to do right or wrong.

4. *It is not right to do wrong in order to do right.* There is a popular untruth going around: "As long as you have a chance to do good, anything goes." This is not true! Right should rise and fall on its own self, not upon the opportunities it presents. The doing of right is an opportunity. The doing of right is its own result, gives its own reward, presents its own satisfaction, and should be done even if it causes one to lose his job, lose his popularity, lose his friends, or lose his all. Right will always turn out right in the end.

Do you remember what happened to Daniel? He was promoted to the top. Nero did wrong and Paul did right. Now people name their boys "Paul" and their dogs "Nero." Stephen did right and died, but he looked up and saw the glory of God and Jesus standing on the right hand of God. John did right and was exiled on the Isle of Patmos, but it turned out right because he saw the great Revelation. The Hebrew children did right, and it looked bad for awhile until the fourth Person came into the fiery furnace and Jesus walked with them.

There is absolutely no thrill comparable to the thrill of doing what is right. Do right if it is unpopular. Do right if it looks bad. Do right if it turns out wrong. Do right when opportunity is lost. Do right if nobody thinks you ought to do right. Do right if nobody else does right. Preachers, do right. Businessmen, do right. College students, do right. Children, do right. Teen-agers, do right. Let everyone that has breath, do right!

Of course, it is not always easy to say "NO!" to wrong, but we must remember that it is always wrong to do wrong and always right to do right. Looking back over my youth I recall three vital times in my life when, thank God, I said, "NO!"

"No" to Drink
One night I was with the wrong crowd. I was a senior. I

thought I was popular, but I wasn't really. I found out later
what it was. I was just the boy that hadn't been with the girls
yet, and I was in the wrong crowd. I had never been out past
eleven o'clock except to sit and think across the street from
our little apartment.

Six of us in a car stopped in front of the Texas Theatre at
one o'clock in the morning. The driver got out a bottle of
whiskey or wine, took a drink, and passed it to the second
person, etc. Each of them took a drink. I was behind the
driver so it got to me last. Yes, they passed it to me! That
was the test. What would I do with it?

(Now right there, young friend, when that decision comes,
the road you take will largely determine what you really are
and what you will do in life.)

I didn't want to be a stick in the mud. After all, suddenly
I was in the gang. I had never been in the gang before. The
girls were taking a second look at me, and all of a sudden (I
didn't know why) they wanted to go with me. I didn't want
to lose the popularity that I had gained. I reached out and
accepted the bottle of wine. I put it an inch from my lips. An
arrow stuck through my heart and I threw the bottle to the
floor! It spilled on everyone in the car. I shouted at the top
of my voice, "TAKE ME HOME!" I was within one inch of
an awful night.

They said, "What? Take you home? Why?"

Never mind why. I am not going to drink it. I promised
God that I wouldn't and I won't."

They said, "Oh, you want to go home and knit, do you?"

I said, "Okay, I will go home and knit, but take me
home."

"Little Sissy wants to go home and embroider and
crochet."

I said, "Okay, I will go home and embroider and crochet,
but take me home!"

They took me to 2632 Idaho and let me out, laughing at
me. By that time it was one-thirty. I walked up the sidewalk,
ashamed to walk in. We lived in a little apartment with two
big trees out in front. The screen door was shut and locked,
and the main door was open. We had a wood stove in the

front room. We had a linoleum floor with very simple, poor furnishings.

My mother was kneeling beside the stove. I stopped and listened to her while she prayed. This was her prayer: "Dear God, I have tried to rear Jack to be a good boy. I have had to be a mother and a father to him. I don't know where he is tonight. He has never been out this late. Dear God, keep him clean. Keep him pure. Help him to remember what I have taught him."

I said, "Mama."

She jumped up, ran to the door, and embraced me.

I said, "Hi, Mama."

Mama said, "Son, you didn't do anything wrong, did you?"

I said, "No." Then I told her that shortly before the bottle was just an inch from my lips. (By the way, thanks be to God, a bottle has never touched these lips, nor has there ever been a cigarette in these lips.)

My mother said, "Son, what time was it?"

I repeated, "Mother, it was one o'clock."

She said, "It was one o'clock when I knelt beside the stove to pray."

Mothers, you can't beat the old-fashioned way of rearing kids by saying, "No-No-No-No! Bad-Bad-Bad-Bad!" Then after you have done all you can, stay on your knees and ask God to help them do right. You can't beat that!

"No" to a Movie

My senior year in high school was a year of decisions. I had a pal who had been my best buddy for quite some time. He and I were together all of the time. We took every course in high school together but one. In 39 classes out of forty he sat right beside me. We were about the same size, and maybe we even looked a little alike.

When graduation time came, my pal and I planned a double date. The four of us attended the baccalaureate on Sunday morning. It was held in a church building. (This was back in the days when we had some religion and decency in America.) After the baccalaureate service we went out to eat and then attended an Open House being held in honor of two of our classmates. However, after we left the Open House there was nothing to do.

My pal said, "What are we going to do tonight?"

I said, "What church shall we go to?"

He said, "Church?"

I said, "Yea."

He said, "Not church! This is Senior Day."

I said, "It is also Sunday."

He said, "Now look, Jack, we have been to church all of our lives. I go to church as much as you do, but this is not the day to go to church." He continued, "let's go to a night club. Let's not drink, but let's just go to a night club."

I said, "GOOD NIGHT, NO!"

He said, At least let's go to a movie."

I said, "No, I am not going to go."

My date looked at me and said, "Boy, what did I draw?"

I said, "I guess you drew a dud."

My pal said, "Okay, we will just take Jack home." They took me home. I called my date's mother and told her that I was no longer responsible for her daughter, and I told her where they were going. The three of them went to a movie, and I went to church. (That is one reason why I make a big to-do about young people who do what is right!) My pastor was so proud of me. My mother was so proud. She would look at her friends as I sat beside her and pointing at me, she would whisper, "He is here."

I felt like I had discovered America. What I didn't know then was that I chose to be a preacher that night. My pal and I had never been apart before. My heart was broken. He went to the movies, and I went to church. I became a preacher. He became a Hollywood actor and producer. I am still in church, and he is still in the movies.

You don't know, young people, what the decisions you make will do to your life. When you say to some boy that is about to put his wicked, vile, sensual paws on you, "Take me home," and you slap him across the face or get a shoe and knock him in the head with it, you never know but what that may be the thing that changes your whole life.

"No" to the Sunday Evening Ball Game

Sports have always interested me greatly. I loved to play ball. I played softball on a city team. I was the only teen-ager on the city league team. The other players were grown men and some were even professional players. A firm gave me a job just so I would play ball for them. I was their pitcher, and they did not have another. We advanced to the championship game. This was a tremendous honor.

We always played our games on Monday, Tuesday, Thursday, Friday, or Saturday nights, but they announced the state championship game would be played on Sunday night at seven o'clock. I had a battle. I will never forget it. It was the biggest thing in my life. For days I battled. What would I do?

The team said, "Why, you have to play. We do not have any other pitcher."

The coach of our team said, "Jack, I am going to go. What is wrong with it? This happens just once in a lifetime. It is the state championship game!"

So I went out and sat under the tree in our yard all Sunday afternoon. I had not made my decision during the previous week.

Someone said to me, "Jack, it won't hurt you."

To this I replied, "It won't hurt you, but it will hurt me if I play."

I made my decision on my knees under the shade of that tree to go on to church that night. When I got to church, the manager had the entire team dressed in uniform and sitting across the street from the church. They tried to talk me into going with them. I was the only hope they had. They didn't have another pitcher. I had pitched three or four no-hit games. Often I would strike out ten to twenty batters a game. They didn't have another pitcher.

They got out of the car, got around me, and said, "Jack, we just have to have you. If you played short stop, it would be different. If you played left field, or center field, or if you were catcher, it would be different, but we do not have any more pitchers. We will be swamped!"

As I walked into the church, two or three of the players

were cursing me. (By the way, they lost the game, 10 to 0.)

My, how I thank God that I had a mighty good mother, a mighty good preacher, and some mighty good Sunday School teachers who cared about me and gave me some principles by which I could live or die!

Years passed. I became a pastor of one church, then another, then another. I was preaching one night at the Junius Heights Baptist Church in Dallas, Texas. When I finished, a middle-age man walked up and said, "Jack Hyles, put 'er there."

I said, "How do you do, sir."

He said, "Do you know me?"

I said, "No, I don't. I am sorry, but I don't."

He said, "You are a pastor now. My, I heard you preach a while ago, and that was great! I used to play for the professional teams, and I was the second baseman on the team for which you pitched."

I said, "You old rascal!"

He said, "Jack, do you remember the time that we played the championship game?"

I thought, "Oh, oh, here it comes right now."

He said, "I cursed you when you walked into the church building, but as I drove to the game that night, I said to myself, 'I wish I had what that kid has.' Jack, I never got away from it. I got what you had in just a few days. I was saved because you didn't pitch that game." Then he said, "I am chairman of the board of deacons at this church."

It always pays to do right!

Chapter Eight

MARY MAGDALENE

Who loved Jesus the most? I guess it is impossible to be dogmatic about this, and yet I would like to nominate Mary Magdalene. Oh, the argument could be presented concerning John, the beloved. Others would vote for the impetuous Peter. Perhaps votes would be cast for James, Andrew, and others. To this author, however, no person during the personal ministry of Christ had the devotion and love for Him as Mary Magdalene. She seems to have been more loyal and more faithful than the others, and our Lord seemed to give her privileges that others did not enjoy.

Why this great devotion? Of course, the answer must lie in the fact that God gave it to her. How was it developed and nourished? No one knows. There are those who think that she was a fallen woman, yet the Scripture gives no verification of this fact. She was possessed of seven devils, the Bible says, but what devils are bigger than malice, envy, etc? There is absolutely no proof that she was a woman of the street, a prostitute, or a harlot. Perhaps she was; perhaps she wasn't. Who knows? Yet one thing is certain: She was really devoted to the Lord Jesus Christ! Let us examine her and her devotion.

1. *She became more than saved.* How tragic it is that so many just get saved and that is all. We should want to have the most devotion possible for our Lord. Nothing but our best should be offered to Him. Mary Magdalene could not stop at just being saved or just being a good Christian. She wanted complete devotion given to her Christ.

2. *Her devotion happened suddenly.* She springs on us in the Bible without warning. Those who have true friendships know that this is often the case. The kind of friend that would die for another finds that it often happens suddenly. The soul is suddenly knit. The tie is suddenly made. It is inexplainable, yet it is there. This, no doubt, means that God does it. How sacred this makes such devotion, such friendship.

38

3. *She cared for the physical needs of Christ.* Luke 8:1-3 finds her being a servant. No sacrifice is too great; no gift is too precious; no task is too difficult when such devotion exists. Let us follow Mary Magdalene and examine her devotion. When Jesus died on the cross, we find she is still His servant, administering to His needs. It was Mary Magdalene who leaned against the sepulchre after He was buried. She came to the garden to pay respects to her Master. For references notice Matthew 27:55 & 61; 28:1, and John 20:11.

It is also interesting to know that our Lord appeared to Mary Magdalene first after His resurrection. Why did Jesus appear to her first? Your imagination could fancy that it was because she would be the happiest to see Him, and happy she was. Why was not this honor reserved for Peter, James, John, or another? It is the opinion of this writer that Mary was His most devoted follower. How beautiful that the supreme devotion should be given, not by the chosen twelve or one of the favorite few, but by a humble, grateful lady who simply would not be denied and who stayed by her Master to the end and even after the end.

4. *She knew His soul.* It is a very interesting thing to know this story concerning Jesus and Mary Magdalene immediately following the resurrection. She supposes she is talking to the gardener as she converses with Christ. He then says one word, "Mary." She then said, "Master." There was something about the way He said, "Mary." There was a soul relationship that existed. Remember that the disciples on the road to Emmaus walked for miles and recognized Christ only when He opened their eyes. The disciples fished for a long time and conversed with Christ at some length before they recognized Him. Leave it to Mary to know Him first. She did not recognize Him by His resurrection body, but her soul had experienced too much fellowship with His not to recognize Him by the way He said, "Mary." How beautiful.

5. *Her devotion did not stop at death.* Her devotion was too great for that. It continued on past His death, and we find her leaning against the sepulchre of her buried Lord. In these days of selfishness and coldness, it is wonderful to

stumble occasionally across a relationship that is built upon the spiritual rather than the physical. Nothing, not even death, can stop such a relationship.

6. *She was as close as His family.* *"Now there stood by the cross of Jesus His mother and His mother's sister, Mary the wife of Cleophas, and Mary Magdalene." (John 19:25)* When Jesus came to death, His mother and his closest friends gathered around the cross. They were not all members of the family.

See Mary Magdalene. She is true to the end. Maybe she knew Him better than others. Maybe she loved Him more. Who knows? Votes for the most devoted follower of Christ would be cast for many different New Testament characters. I vote for Mary Magdalene.

Chapter Nine

FOR SALE

One's degree of character may be determined by what he would do wrong, for so many are so prone to "sell out" so soon. Politicians, preachers, and others find the temptation to sell out to be a great one. Some sell for much and some sell for little.

The tendency to be for sale starts in childhood. If the child is not taught that wrong is punished, and if he gets no spankings, wrong is not made distasteful to him. He oftentimes gets his desires by doing wrong. If he cries long enough, he gets the candy, and oftentimes he is even rewarded when throwing a temper tantrum. He does not have to mind his parents. To say "no" to Mama is considered cute. Then he will say "no" to the teacher, "no" to the Sunday School worker, "no" to the law, and "no" to God. He then dies and goes to Hell because the parents thought it was cute for him to say "no."

This tendency to sell out continues in youth. It is found in the youth who does right only if it turns out right. Right needs to be vindicated in such a life. Every action is determined by its reward or results. According to this opinion, nothing is right or wrong in itself, only in how it turns out. Hence, anything can become right if it turns out right. Popularity, gaining a new boy friend, good grades, etc. become the main end rather than principles and character. How sad! Such people stand only until the price is big enough. They are not taught to live by principles. Their convictions last only until the selling price reaches their desires.

This tendency increases in adulthood. From such young people we have our police scandals, our crooked politicians, our compromising preachers, our loafers, lawbreakers, and homebreakers.

Early in childhood our youth should be taught the need for conviction and that right is its own reward and needs no vindication. They should be taught never to sell out for convenience or fair price, but rather to place a sign over their souls, "Not for Sale."

Chapter Ten

PERSONALITY PRIORITIES

One of the most important Scriptures in the Bible for a Christian is found in II Peter 1:5. *"And beside this, giving all diligence, add to your faith virtue; and to virtue knowledge."* Here the Holy Spirit inspires Peter to list for us some virtues necessary for character. Notice in verse 5 the words "add to." These words come from the singing of an old Grecian song. The custom was for the people to join their hands as they sang. This means that the following virtues are to "join hands" in the Christian's life, and they are to do so in the proper order.

1. *Diligence.* This word could be translated "hastening to do a thing well." It is doing the job well, and it is doing the job swiftly. There is a false teaching going around that people who do things swiftly do not do them well, and that people who do things slowly are of necessity thorough. This is not true. We should be diligent; every task should be done well; but we should do it in the least time possible so we can do *more* for God. Hence, we have the first stone laid. This is the stone of diligence.

2. *Faith.* Once the stone of diligence has been laid, faith should be placed on top of it. Notice there is no need for faith without diligence, for faith without works is dead. Just to have faith in what God is going to do is not enough. We are to be willing to do our best. *God will not do what we can do, but He will do what we cannot do after we have done what we can do.* What is faith? Faith is the belief in what God has done, what God can do, what God will do, what God is going to do, and what God is going to use *me* to do. I have said so often that a Christian should make no provision for failure. Faith is basically *"I can do all things through Christ which strengtheneth me."*

3. *Virtue.* Next in line we have this trait. Now it is interesting that so far nothing has been mentioned about kindness. That will come later. Far more important than

kindness is diligence, faith, and virtue. Honesty is better than courtesy. *It is better to do right wrongly than to do wrong rightly. Position is more important than disposition. Integrity is better than popularity. Being a right fellow is more important than being a "regular" fellow.* Do not misunderstand. It is important to be kind. Courtesy is important. The right spirit is important. Disposition is important. Being a nice person is important. However, these should never be placed above such traits as virtue.

Many years ago when I first began preaching I faced a big decision in my ministry. My heart was broken. My face was against the wall. I then made five promises to God and established five principles that have governed my life ever since.

a. *If I have a friend, I will stick with him.*

b. *I will base my decisions on right or wrong, not on how right or wrong turn out.*

c. *No one will tamper with my preaching. I will ask only God what I shall preach and where I preach.*

d. *I will never seek a raise or talk money.*

e. *I will treat the rich and poor alike.*

One should live by principle, not by convenience. *When principles are established early in life, fewer decisions have to be made later. The principles make the decisions for us, and hence, frustration is averted and avoided.*

4. *Wisdom.* For many years my prayer list has been topped with power, love, and wisdom. Wisdom is certainly one of the great personality priorities. Notice it comes before self control, godliness, brotherly kindness, or love. Remember that God has given us a divine order. The bricks are laid one at a time on top of each other. First should be laid diligence, then faith, then virtue, then wisdom.

Wisdom is the ability to use knowledge. It is available to all. *"If any of you lack wisdom, let him ask of God, that giveth to all men liberally, and upbraideth not; and it shall be given him." (James 1:5)*

5. *Self control.* This is the next brick in the wall. It precedes godliness, kindness, and love. Self control means discipline. It means discipline over body appetites such as

eating and sex. It includes the disciplining of one's schedule, mind, disposition, emotions, frustrations, etc. Nothing will take its place. It is vital to the life of the Christian.

6. *Godliness, kindness, and love.* Now we are coming to the traits that show. God starts on the inside and works out. He starts with the foundation and works up. No one can see wisdom, virtue, and faith; but we cannot have true godliness until these stones have been laid. We cannot have Bible kindness until these stones have been laid. We cannot have real love until these stones have been laid. Love is one of the great attributes a Christian can have. Kindness, of course, is important. Godliness is vital, but a godliness, a kindness, or a love that is not built from the inside will not last. It will be superficial. If one gains diligence and adds to it faith; to faith, virtue; to virtue, wisdom; to wisdom, self control; then godliness, kindness, and love will of necessity come.

Let us teach our children and teach ourselves the proper order of character and its priorities. Let us use God's order. To teach them to be kind, and yet not make them obey is folly. To teach them to be loving, and yet not teach them self control is foolishness. Let us exercise care in trying to place all of these things in our lives. Let us give the proper emphasis where God gives the emphasis. All across our country we find a bankruptcy of character. We are more interested in "nice guys" than "right guys." We are more interested in being friendly than being a friend, and in having a good disposition rather than having the right position.

In politics, in the ministry, and in business there is a desperate need for people who have character. Personality is important; talent is important; but a good personality with talent will oftentimes run from character. The motto of some seems to be, "Why work hard? I have it made. I can talk my way out of it." On the other hand, a child that is taught to have character will get the necessary talent. Talent oftentimes flees character. Character will always seek talent — that is, the talent necessary to fulfill the task. How vital it is that we stress character and place each of its qualities in the proper order.

Chapter Eleven

I CORINTHIANS 10:13 – ALL THE SAME

"There hath no temptation taken you but such as is common to man: but God is faithful, Who will not suffer you to be tempted above that ye are able; but will with the temptation also make a way to escape, that ye may be able to bear it." (I Corinthians 10:13)

The other day a question was asked which often is directed my way: "Why don't you get mad at your enemies? How is it that you are sometimes able to avoid retaliation and revenge?" My answer invariably is I Corinthians 10:13. Such thoughts as these that follow are a constant source of help in overcoming bitterness, vindication, retaliation, and revenge.

1. *All people have the same attributes.* Yes, I certainly think that the Apostle Paul had the same temptations that I have. Our temptations are common to man. If this be true, I have in me what I don't like in you, and these same ingredients are found in the life of every person. To be sure, different amounts of certain sins or temptations may exist in different people, but the fact remains, I have in me what I don't like in you. Hence, I must be tolerant toward you.

2. *Each asset has a liability, and each liability has an asset.* In other words, with the asset of purity, often comes the liability of Phariseeism. With the asset of friendliness often comes the liability of compromise. With the asset of leadership often comes the liability of pride. This philosophy levels each of us with his neighbor. It eliminates pride. A characteristic which is good about us carries with it the temptation for something bad. Negatively, a bad characteristic often carries a tendency toward an asset. One who is stubborn may develop conviction. One who is proud may have the asset of leadership. One who is guilty of Phariseeism may carry with him the asset of purity. Seeing such equality in the human race will avoid over-exaltation

and excessive criticism of one's fellow man.

If the above be consistently true, and perhaps it is not, and if we love people because of what they are, we will find ourselves loving all people, for all have in them what all others have in them.

3. *If we then love one person more than the other, the love is given to us by God.* This is a great thought. If you have a friend who lives by this philosophy and loves you more than he does others, it is because God gave him that love. Think of the security involved. It is not generated, human love or man-made affection, it is love given from God by His grace, and, consequently, will not change.

Think what such a philosophy does for one: It eliminates criticism in this life. It encourages the impure to realize that even the pure possess impurity. Remember that no temptations take us but such as are common to man. This theory will also humble the pure, for the pure will find in himself liabilities and temptations that will make him more careful to undergird himself against Satan's wiles.

This also offers real humility and meekness. It makes one think of himself as no better or worse than anyone else. It will help to eliminate both inferiority and superiority complexes.

If each of us will examine his assets, he will no doubt find the temptations that each asset carries. This will drive each of us to more dependence upon God and His help and strength.

As one grows in this grace and in all Christian graces he will find himself being more and more alone in society. Someone has said there is a fine line of distinction between a genius and a moron. This appears to be so because each is about the same distance from society or from the masses. The truth, however, is that the only similarity a genius and a moron have is their distance from the average. They are really on the opposite ends of the pole. The same thing is true concerning true love and lust. Love and lust look alike only because the masses would be the same distance from both. Love and lust are on the opposite ends of the pole, but since we interpret everything according to what we think, we associate the two together because they are both the same distance from the masses.

The more we become like Christ, the farther we will travel from Mr. Average. Mr. Average is the one who gives us our reputation for being a good person. The one who grows the most in grace, the one who loves the most, the one who sacrifices the most, the one who gives the most will probably be looked upon by society as being as obnoxious as the one at the other end of the line. Hence, the one who is Christlike will not appear to be Christlike to the world. In contrast, one who appears to be Christlike, no doubt, has missed Christlikeness.

Let each of us realize that the weaknesses of his neighbor are found in some degree in ourselves. Hence, because what is found in all of us is in the rest of us, it behooves none of us to be critical, for in the final analysis we are all depraved creatures with common temptations and common weaknesses. In criticizing our neighbor, we are criticizing ourselves, for we have a common origin.

Chapter Twelve

GREATNESS

"For whosoever will save his life shall lose it: and whosoever will lose his life for My sake shall find it." Matthew 16:25.

A few days ago in my study I was meditating on the above Scripture when the thought came to me that the only lasting thing one can ever get for himself comes from the leftovers when he gives to others. The strange paradox of the Christian life is that the way up is down; the way forward is backward; and the way to be served is to serve.

This is especially true concerning friendship. It is infinitely better to be a friend than to have a friend. It is better to become something than to obtain something. When one becomes a friend, he will, no doubt, have friends. (Of course, this should not be his motive, or he too will fail.) No one ever found a friend searching for a friend, but many have stumbled upon lasting friendships while being a friend. One should forget whether or not he has friends and concentrate on being the right kind of friend.

The same is true concerning happiness. No one ever charted a plan for personal happiness who found it, but millions have found happiness in the pathway of carrying out responsibilities. Oftentimes people come to my office and say, "Pastor, how can I find happiness?"

I invariably say, "Forget it. Think of the happiness of others. There are so many who have problems so much worse than you. Forget your own happiness. Seek to make others happy, and one day you will return to me and say, 'Pastor, in my effort to make others happy, I suddenly, to my surprise, found that I have become happy too!' "

This same truth can be applied to peace of mind. It seems nowadays that in order for a magazine to sell, it must have an article about sex and another about peace of mind. No one can tell anyone else how to have peace of mind, and no one can set out to find peace of mind and find it. When one, however, forgets himself and becomes obsessed with the needs of others,

49

he suddenly realizes he has peace.

Several years ago a lady came to my office stating that she was fearing an imminent nervous breakdown. I suggested that each day she do something for someone else. "Bake cookies and take them to a friend one day," I suggested. "The next day take some roses to the hospital and give a rose to each patient who has no visitor during visiting hours. The next day drop by and see a blind person. The next day take a cake to one of our deaf friends and simply write the words, 'I love you,' on a card. Continue this indefinitely," I said, "and see if it helps."

Months passed. One day I asked the lady about her proposed nervous breakdown. (It seems that most of the ladies I know are either having a nervous breakdown, just getting over one, or planning one real soon.) "How about that nervous breakdown?" I asked.

"Oh Pastor," she said, "I just got so busy doing things for other people that I had to postpone it." (She had found the answer.)

I think it was R. A. Torrey who came in one day after a preaching mission and hurriedly began preparations for another trip. He had some dirty clothes he needed to have laundered. He asked a young friend if he could take care of this for him.

"What? Do you think I am an errand boy?" said the young friend.

Another young friend stood by who overheard the conversation. "Let me do it," he exclaimed.

The young man did take care of the menial task for R. A. Torrey. His name? Oh, his name was James M. Gray, who one day became the president of Moody Bible Institute.

When we think of success or greatness, we think of giving commands and being obeyed. When we think of greatness, we think of having much. When Jesus thought of greatness, He thought of giving much. When we think of greatness, we think of being served. When Jesus thought of greatness, He thought of serving.

A poll was once conducted in the country of France to determine the greatest Frenchman who ever lived. The experts unanimously predicted, of course, that Napoleon would win by a landslide. The poll was won by a landslide all right, but not by Napoleon, but rather by none other than Louis Pasteur. Once again the servant had won over the served. The giver had won over the receiver, and he who lost his life had found it.

Let us remember that the only thing one can ever obtain for himself comes from the leftovers after he gives to others.

Chapter Thirteen

DEEPENING RELATIONSHIPS

On a recent weekday morning I was speaking in a church in the city where I grew up. I had moved there when I was only one year old. There I attended elementary school, junior high school, and high school. I was faithful to my church as a child. I had pastored in the same county for nearly seven years. I had helped to start sixteen churches in the area, and twelve of my preacher boys are now pastoring nearby. In spite of this, there were less than a hundred people in the morning service, and to my knowledge not one from the church where I grew up and only two from the church where I pastored for seven years.

"Don't they love me?" I asked.

"Why, of course, they do," was the answer that came to my mind. It is just the fact that they did not love me as much as I loved them. Perhaps this is just another case of deep love being unreturned.

What causes us to have such little depth of love? Perhaps there are several reasons:

1. *Most love is simply the satisfying of an appetite.* People normally come to hear a person speak because they want to see him or because they want to hear him. If they have heard him recently, why should they hear him again? We seldom think about the satisfying of the appetites of others. We are basically concerned about the satisfying of our own appetites. This, of course, is not deep love. In some sense, it is lust in that it is to satisfy an appetite.

2. *Most love must be generated by an atmosphere.* A beautiful moon at night, soft music in the background, the faint smell of perfume, etc. not only are helpful but oftentimes necessary to most love. *Real love loves at all times, at noonday as well as midnight, and whether the odor is Chanel No. 5 or "Perspiration No. 6."*

As a boy I went with a girl whom I liked very much. One night we were walking together looking at the moon when she said, "Doesn't that moon make you feel romantic?"

I answered, "Yes."

She talked about the moon for thirty minutes. (I think she was in love with the Moon.) I felt like shouting, "How about me?" The moon is only a visual aid.

I have often said that when I love someone I love them as much on the Dan Ryan Expressway in downtown Chicago as I do on a lonely road with a beautiful moon.

3. *Most love becomes disinterested when acquired.* Here is a tragic truth. It is the acquiring of the relationship that many people want rather than the having of the relationship. Many marriages fail because the acquiring of the relationship is more important than the relationship itself. The same is true with friendships. The acquiring of a relationship is certainly not the ending but just the beginning. It is the commencement. Real character is never satisfied with its depth.

4. *Much love knows no degree or availability of depth.* One should think of the great possibilities of the depth of love. God is love. In Him is perfect love. The difference between the love I have today and the love He has is the potential for the growth and depth of my love. It is not "in love and out of love." It is not simply love or no love. When one learns to love, he enters into a world of possibilities, growth, and depth.

Upon returning from the morning service mentioned in the first paragraph is this chapter someone asked, "Doesn't that make you sad? Isn't it heartbreaking when people do not love you as much as you love them?"

My answer was an emphatic "no" for several reasons as found below:

a. *The line between positive and negative should be very low.* It should take very little to please us, and it should take much to displease us. We should find our satisfaction in loving, not being loved. Our joys should be wrapped up in the giving, not the receiving.

b. *It is good to take a trip; it is better to have a partner.* Notice I did not say it is good to take a trip with a partner, but bad to go alone. It is not a matter of good or bad, but good or better. Hence, if a friend's love for you does not increase, it will not keep your love from deepening. Believe me, *it is better for you to love alone than not to love at all.* If one has to take the trip of depth alone, it is not as good as sharing it with another, but it is infinitely better than not knowing the depth.

c. *Sometimes a relationship comes that reciprocates.* When this happens, it turns good into better. Bear in mind that it does not turn bad into good. To have love is good; to have love that is reciprocated is better.

d. *Such relations let us look into the mind of God.* When we love and it is not returned, we know something of His great heart of love. He so seldom finds reciprocation. When we do find a relationship where love is reciprocated, we know something of how God feels when He finds someone who loves Him with all his heart. Bear in mind that the purpose of God's creating man was that man might love and fellowship with God. Though God is grieved when His love is not returned, He nevertheless does not withdraw His love. How happy He must be, however, when one of His creatures returns His love.

e. *The more lonely we become, the less lonely He becomes.* The deeper a person grows in his love the more he is separated from the rest of mankind. In that separation, however, he becomes more like Christ and he finds he can offer Christ pure fellowship. When we grow in grace and in love and find ourselves misunderstood and lonely, we look around and find that Christ has been there all of the time. He is happy to see us. Then, and only then, can we offer Him the love for which He yearns. Since His love is so unlike our love, when our love becomes like His love, our love will become less like the love of man. As it becomes less like the love of man, it becomes more like the love of God. As it becomes more like the love of God, it gives us the ability to help satisfy the travail of His soul.

f. *This is the kind of love that does not stop when it cannot be reciprocated.* This love does not forget the pretty when it becomes ugly. It does not forget the young when it becomes old. It does not forget the rich when it becomes poor. It "never faileth."

OBSERVATIONS

1. *I want to keep lovable.* Since most people know nothing about deep love, but rather tend to seek that which satisfies the appetite, I would then attempt to keep in my personality and character the things for which the appetites crave. For example, if a person is hungry to hear a fresh message, I would want to provide that fresh message. If a person is hungry to be with a friendly soul, I would want to be that friendly soul. Just because another's love is not as deep as mine should not keep me from attempting to satisfy his wholesome and holy appetites. In other words, I want to keep having what they need. No doubt, hundreds of people come to hear us preachers simply because we have what they need. They do not come because they deeply love us; they come because they love to hear us. If this be true, we should have what they need.

2. *I can thank God that I am where I am and not where they are.* It is infinitely better to be the lover than the loved. It is better to offer love unreciprocated than it is to fail to reciprocate love offered you.

3. *May I never be a mental or physical invalid.* This is a strange thought, but a true one. How tragic it would be to lose the ability to love. Then how tragic it would be to retain that ability but lose the ability to help those whom you love. Hence, I must keep my mind healthy so I can love my friends. I must keep my body healthy so that I can help my friends.

Perhaps the most underrated word in the English language is "friend." *He is "just a friend," we often say. That is like saying that eternity is "just forever" or that the ocean is "just a pond."* Let us pray God to give us depth of love and depth of relationship even if that depth is unreciprocated. There is little doubt in my mind that in God's mercy He will, in His own time and will, give us a relationship or relationships that do reciprocate.

Chapter Fourteen

PREMATURE NOSTALGIA

How many times it has been said, "I didn't know how much I loved her," or "I wish I had done more while he was alive." How sad are such statements. Instead of "I wish I had done it," why not substitute something like this: "I will wish I had done it so I will now do it; then I will not have to wish that I had done it." Look toward the future to the day when you will lose a relationship. Picture yourself without it; become prematurely nostalgic, and you will appreciate the relationship more in the present. This eliminates remorse, and remorse is the sting of nostalgia.

In Ecclesiastes 12:1 we have a man whose life had been lived with much of it being lived foolishly. Looking back over his life he had remorse. Let us notice how to take remorse out of the future.

1. *Do everything on purpose.* Say what you mean and mean what you say. Discipline the mind to control the emotions and the actions. Far too often we are prone to say things we do not mean. We do things caused by temporary emotional stimuli. We then find ourselves sorry in the future for our behavior. Because of this, one's mind and actions should be so disciplined that he will do everything on purpose. Hence, he leaves no room for remorse in the future.

2. *Make relationships the most important thing in life.* It is easy to use the patients to build a hospital, to use the pupils to build a school, and to use a family to keep a clean house. The purpose of a house is to care for the children. The purpose for the school is to educate the pupil. The purpose of the hospital is to heal the patient. The individual is all important! Therefore, one should see to it that relationships in life are more important than anything else. Relationships should be nourished and cultivated. They should not be made or perpetuated haphazardly. If human relationships have the proper places in our lives, then we will give more diligence and care to the treatment of our fellowman, thereby eliminating future remorse.

3. *Do not "weigh" a person every day.* Someone said, "I have changed my opinion about him." Then he should not have had an opinion. The person is what he was yesterday. He has not changed. The opinion was in error. The simple truth is that one does not have to have an opinion about people. If no opinion is formed, or if a careful, accurate, and objective opinion is formed, then the opinion will not have to be changed, and we will not be disappointed to find that a friend is imperfect.

4. *Plan every relationship carefully.* Each person has a few basic relationships in life. For example, I am a son, a husband, a father, a brother, and a friend. I must look carefully at these relationships and plan to be my best in each one. For example, for many years I planned to be a father. As a child, I looked forward to being a dad. My relationship as a dad has been one that has been calculated and planned with much prayer.

It is unbelievable, yet true, that we spend less time preparing for life's most important relationships. The theologian may spend seven to ten years in preparation. The medical doctor may spend even more than that. The school teacher spends many years in preparation, but the sad truth is that many of us spend little or no time preparing to be a wife, husband, brother, sister, mother, father, or friend. Each of us should become an expert in being what he should be in each of life's relationships. Much study, thought, and care should be exercised in becoming the best that one can become in each relationship of life. If such relationships are carefully planned, and if we do our best in becoming what we should become, then we will have no cause for remorse in years to come. If we do not do our best to become the best in every relationship, we may well spend many hours filled with remorse because we did not become all that we could have become to those who loved us.

5. *Make every experience with every relationship a sacred one.* Life is so brief, and no experience can be recalled. Because of this fact, each experience should be squeezed to its fullest. If we make the most of every relationship of life, and if we make the most of every experience of life's

relationships, then there will be no remorse in days to come concerning failures. If we lackadaisically and haphazardly go through life not realizing the importance of our relationships and the depth of our experiences, we will wake up one day realizing the hours, days and years that were wasted, at least, partially, because the mind did not absorb the depth of life's experiences. Someday we will look back upon them and find that we did not take advantage of them. This causes remorse.

Yes, we should have premature nostalgia. *We should look out into the future and predict what things could bring us remorse. We then should predict what causes such remorse and should set about immediately to eliminate them in the present and avoid the remorse in the future.*

Chapter Fifteen

GRATITUDE

"And He looked up, and saw the rich men casting their gifts into the treasury." (Luke 21:1)

"And it came to pass, as He went to Jerusalem, that He passed through the midst of Samaria and Galilee." (Luke 17:11)

Real gratitude is real humility. One cannot be humble without gratitude, and one cannot be grateful without humility. Many years ago someone took a poll as to the greatest sin committed by mankind. To the surprise of many, the sin chosen as the greatest and most oft committed was the sin of ingratitude. Let us meditate for a while upon this grace which is so necessary to a successful and happy Christian life.

1. *There is no such thing as a self-made man.* We often hear it said of someone that he is self-made. Nothing could be farther from the truth. Each of us is largely a product of the influences of others. One cannot divorce himself from the contributions that others have made to his life. Short-sighted and self-centered is the person who does not regularly recognize the contributions that others have made to his life, his success, and his stature.

Paul said, *"For we cannot but speak the things which we have seen and heard." (Acts 4:20)*

2. *The foundation of gratitude is the expectation of nothing.* One should remember that though he is debtor to all men, he should feel that none are indebted to him. Not only is this one of the secrets to possessing gratitude, but also it is one of the secrets to happiness. If one expects nothing, then anything is a bonus. If one expects more than he receives, he is disappointed. If he expects less than he receives, he will be pleased even though what he receives is the same.

3. *Weigh a small gift.* We are so prone to judge the size of a gift by how much it costs. This is certainly a poor basis for measurement. *Money is simply time wrapped in a paper sack.*

59

The man who makes a dollar an hour gives as much when he gives a dollar as does the man who makes fifty dollars an hour and gives fifty dollars. Didn't Jesus say that the woman who gave two mites had given more than them all?

On my last birthday I received many wonderful gifts. Which was the greatest? I am not sure, but it may have been the gift given me by a small lad. After I had baptized on a Sunday evening I was met at the door by a Junior boy who had made a birthday card and taped two quarters on the bottom of the card for me. This was probably a week's allowance for him, and no doubt he spent a half day drawing childlike pictures on a piece of paper to make his preacher a birthday card. Hence, he gave me seven and a half days of his life as far as money is concerned. Some would have to give a hundred dollars to equal his gift because this is what they would make in seven days. Others would have to give a thousand dollars to equal this fifty-cent gift. As I weighed the size of my birthday gifts, I thought perhaps this boy had given more than them all.

Another gift I received was a birthday cake made by a lady who has a limited amount of money but unlimited love. Now if it took her three hours to make this cake, she gave me as much as anyone if they had given me the amount of money it took them three hours to earn. When one weighs a gift in this light, the gift becomes not small at all, and gratitude can fill the heart.

4. *Do not measure a large gift.* Bear in mind that we are trying to develop gratitude. A large gift is easier to appreciate, and the weighing of such a gift oftentimes decreases gratitude. Hence, we weigh the small gift in order to gain more gratitude, but we do not weigh the large lest it take away from our gratitude.

5. *Never lose appreciation for a gift.* Gratitude acquired should be gratitude kept. Continue to think of the gift. Continue to thank God for the giver. Just to say, "Thank you," one time is not sufficient. Just to reciprocate once is not enough.

When I was a boy my sister made our living for a number of years. My dad was unemployed and the only food we had

was the food provided by my sister. The first new bicycle
that I ever owned was bought by my sister. She bought me
my first baseball glove and fed, clothed, and housed me
during some crucial years. I must not forget this. Just to say,
"Thank you," one time or give an expression of thanks one time
is not sufficient. I must continue to express my gratitude.

6. *Let nothing extinguish gratitude.* There is a strange but
true fact about the human race: We are so prone to complain
because the roses have thorns rather than to rejoice because
the thorns have roses. Someone has said that it hurts more to
have to have your arm cut off than it feels good to have it on.
How tragically true this is. This is the reason that someone
may do a thousand kindnesses for another and yet lose his
"friendship" because of one seeming injustice. A soul winner
can lead another to Christ, point him to Heaven, save him
from an eternity without God or hope, but later do
something to disappoint that convert and strangely and
tragically lose that "friendship." Let us keep our balance.
Don't leave a church because the Pastor who has said
thousands of things to help you says one thing to hurt you.
Do not lose gratitude because someone who has done
something for you seemingly does something against you. Let
nothing extinguish our appreciation and gratitude to those
who have befriended us.

7. *Feel gratitude in the heart and think through every gift
given to you and every gesture done for you.* Think of all of
the possibilities concerning the plans and effort put forth in
the doing of something on your behalf. Let gratitude swell in
your heart as you do.

8. *Be sure to express gratitude.* Our Lord tells the story of
the ten lepers who were cleansed. Only one returned to
express thanks. Jesus asked, "Where are the nine?" Now it is
entirely possible that some of the others felt gratitude, but
failed to express it. There are so many of our feelings and
expressions that go unexpressed, thereby robbing countless
people of blessings. It has been the policy around our house
for many years to encourage our children to express
gratitude. A personal note of appreciation at the end of the
school year to a teacher and a verbal or a written expression

of gratitude to anyone doing a favor or kindness to them could always bring blessing. How important it is that we relay to people the feelings of our hearts in such matters.

9. *Be grateful for the usual. It is easy to be grateful for a bonus; it is character to be grateful for a salary.* Most of us do not appreciate the usual things of life until they are lost. One of the finest ways to develop gratitude for the usual is to have periods set aside to imagine what life would be like if the usual were lost. Sometime each day think of the sorrow of a losing a husband, or wife, or a child, or a pastor, or a church. Such thinking will lead to gratitude in the heart and should lead to open expressions of that gratitude.

10. *Be grateful for the least.* The more you appreciate the little, the more you will enjoy the average. Most of us have much more than we deserve, or for that matter, than anyone in previous generations has ever had. May God give us gratitude to Himself, gratitude to our loved ones, and gratitude to our friends. Then may He give us character to express the feelings of our heart to Him and to those who mean so much to us and do so much for us.

Chapter Sixteen

HOW YOU LOOK AT YOUR LIFE

The roses have thorns and the thorns have roses. Life is made that way. All assets have liabilities, and all liabilities have assets. Those who laugh the most will cry the most. Those who cry the most will laugh the most. Those who love the dearest will suffer the dearest losses, for nothing is permanent in this life, and all must some day be given up. When a child is born, he is born to die. Hence, the joys of the maternity ward will some day be balanced by the tears of the mortuary. If there are a few children, there are fewer finger marks on the walls, fewer sleepless nights, and fewer doctor bills. Perhaps it is true that in the end our joys and sorrows all come out even. If one has few friends, he will lose few friends. The more friends that one has, the more times he will have to go to the cemetery with a broken heart. Since every asset has liabilities and every liability has assets, could it be then that none of us has a worse time than the rest of us? The asset of much money carries with it the liability of shallow friends. The asset of deep love carries with it the possibility of a deeper heartbreak. The more that is acquired, the more that must be lost. If the above be true, there are several lessons that can be learned.

1. *Happiness depends upon whether we magnify the assets or liabilities.* If every asset has a liability and every liability has an asset, if every bad has a good and every good has a bad, and if life's assets and liabilities are all evened out in the end, then each of us has the same possibilities of happiness. Those who look at the liabilities more than the assets become unhappy. Those who magnify the assets over the liabilities become happy. May we rejoice over the having of the child rather than sorrow over the fingerprints on the wall. Far too many are so busy looking at the lost column that they forget it all evens out in the end.

2. *If the above be true, no one has it worse than the other.* Even in our defeats there are lessons we learn that the victorious ones never know. Hence, one has no more right to complain than another.

3. *A realization of this truth will cure envy.* Why envy another if his liabilities match his assets as do ours? He has as much right to envy us.

4. *This truth will make us choose a life that does the most for others.* If the books balance out as we are supposing, then we will come out even regardless. Could it be then that the grasping of this philosophy will lead us to choose the kind of life that will do the most for others? In other words, if there is no way at all that we can gain more assets than liabilities, we may then center our attention on helping others to gain assets.

5. *This truth will take away the desire for personal gain and selfishness.* That thing that you want will bring with it a liability that you may not want to assume. The more things you own, the more things you can break. The more conveniences that one obtains the more repair bills he will have. Hence, we are led simply to say to God, "Give us what You know is best for us, and we will trust Your wisdom and judgment."

6. *This truth will drive us to do the will of God.* If all our attainments and obtainments lead us to the same place, then we must cast ourselves upon the Lord and His will. Nothing else will much matter but that which He wants us to do. If there is no asset that does not bring with it a liability, there can be nothing that we really do want or do not want. If we obtain it, we can rejoice because of its assets. If we do not obtain it, we can thank God for the privilege of not having to accept the liability. So since it is six of one and a half a dozen of another we can turn our eyes toward Jesus and say, "Thy will be done."

Chapter Seventeen

YOU CAN DO WHAT YOU OUGHT TO DO

Once a dear lady on my staff became a bit discouraged because her work seemed more than she was able to do. She had recently accepted her position with us and was somewhat frustrated with her inability to perform all of her new duties. In an effort to help her and the rest of the staff, I presented at staff devotions one Monday morning the following suggestions:

1. *Believe that you can do what you ought to do.* God never gives us anything to do that He does not give us the strength to do. The Apostle Paul reminds us in Philippians 4:13, "*I can do all things through Christ which strengtheneth me.*" When I was a student pastor, a fellow student gave me a wonderful truth when he said, "When God calls, He qualifies." This He does! You *can* do what God has given you to do. You *can* do what you ought to do. You *can* do what you are supposed to do. If this be true, it may be appropriated by faith. Faith is the key that unlocks God's cupboard. Claim for your task the strength that you need to perform it.

2. *Do not un-do in doubt what you have done in faith.* When a job has been accepted in faith, do not un-do it in doubt. When God called me to become Pastor of the First Baptist Church in Hammond, Indiana, He miraculously led me to accept the call. Though I personally did not want to make a change, I was nevertheless assured that God's will was being done. I contacted the church, offering my acceptance. I then gave my resignation to the Miller Road Baptist Church in Garland, Texas, where I had labored for nearly seven years. I gave them a thirty-day notice. During this thirty-day period I became doubtful that I had made the right decision. Emotion gripped my soul as I thought of the heartache of leaving those dear friends. Again and again since that time, God has vindicated that decision and has shown me over and over that it was a wise one.

Has God called you to do a task? He will then equip you for

65

it. Has God led you to a place? He will then qualify you for the job.

3. *Realize that success does not depend upon talent.* The great prerequisite for success is not talent but character. Character seeks talent. Talent often runs from character. The talented man often thinks he can make it on his own. The man of character realizes he cannot make it on his own and must work to equip himself for his job. Integrity, diligence, honesty, and hard work are the main secrets to success. Average public speakers often become more successful preachers than more gifted men. Mediocre singers often accomplish more than ten talented ones. I have often said that in employing secretaries and staff members, I look for traits such as loyalty, tenacity, and integrity, rather than typing, shorthand, and other talents. Because one is a typist does not mean he will have loyalty and character. Because one has character does mean he will learn to type if his job requires it.

4. *Work as hard as you can believing God will do the rest.* God will not do what you can do. Someone has said, "Man's extremity is God's opportunity." A lazy college student who believes God will provide his needs is not living by faith but by folly. A shiftless pastor who believes that God will grow his church has misunderstood the entire meaning of faith. Faith is doing everything I can do, and then trusting God to do what I cannot do. God can do what I cannot do, but He will not do what I can do if I refuse to do it.

5. *After the job is done, give God the glory.* Tragic but true is the fact that many of us fall prostrate before the Lord asking His help before attempting a task, then we bow gracefully and proudly as we hear the applause coming from men after we have accomplished the task. In my own life I started out as a very poor boy. When God called me to be a preacher, I was untalented and unprepared. My first sermon ended in failure and frustration after five minutes of searching for something to say. If successes come, I must not forget those early days. I must remember that I am what I am by the grace of God. I have what I have by the grace of God, and I have done what I have done by the grace of God. *"For I know that in me (that is, in my flesh,) dwelleth no good thing." (Romans 7:18)* It is His

work and not mine. It is done by His Spirit and not mine. Hence, when the victory comes, I must step back in the shadows and say, *"The Lord gave. . .blessed be the Name of the Lord." (Job 1:21)*

Chapter Eighteen

THE CAPACITY TO ENJOY

Recently while sharing with some others a happy time, I said, "Isn't it a wonderful thing to have the capacity for enjoyment?" Many people have never developed such. Their enjoyment is always accompanied by a dissatisfaction because of its brevity, an overemphasis of its liability, or one of a thousand different complexes that immune people from having fun. There are several things that one can do to enhance his chances for enjoyment and to develop a capacity for the same.

1. *Remember that everything is relative.* What can be an enjoyment to one can be a drudgery to another depending upon the plateau of life in which he lives. Two people can eat the same meal. One can enjoy it; the other cannot because one is accustomed to a better standard of living than the other. Hence, it is vitally important for us to compare our present experiences with our darker days rather than our brighter ones. If there were no darkness, there could be no light. If there were no hot, there could be no cold. If there were no low, there could be no high. How high something is depends upon the thing with which we compare it. If one is having a usual experience of life, he can compare it with the best day he ever had and mourn, or he can compare it with the worst day he ever had and rejoice. Since most everything is relative, one should compare an experience with lesser ones that he has had and find joy in what he *is* doing.

2. *Learn to rejoice in sorrow.* The Apostle Paul said that he gloried in his tribulations. The Psalmist said, "They that sow in tears shall reap in joy." So there is a way that a person can be happy in both joy and sorrow. When we are sharing a joyful experience, we are of necessity happy; but when we share a sorrowful experience, we can rejoice in that a tear today is an investment for a laugh tomorrow.

There are other compensations in sorrow. One draws closer to the Lord in such hours. Friends who share life's dark hours become better friends. One's *happiness will not be determined upon how happy he is his happiest day, but how happy he is his saddest day. It is not the height of the mountains but the height of the valleys that determines joy and happiness.* Let us learn to rejoice in our sorrows and count them as investments for rejoicing tomorrow.

3. *One should develop a variety of enjoyments.* Many people have to be hearing jokes to be happy. To be sure, good clean humor is a part of fun, but it is certainly far from all of it, and it is even far from being the most important part of it.

What can beat the enjoyment of a serious conversation when two people share ideas and when two minds meet at a common denominator? Unfortunate is the one for whom the spectacular is necessary for fun.

Recently a group of Christians were on a bus trip together. They had had some spectacular enjoyment. They had laughed until they cried. They had a lot of loud, wonderful, happy fun, but as the trip was nearing its end, it was suggested that everyone sing. They found themselves singing some of the old songs: "When I Was Seeing Nelly Home," "Bicycle Built for Two," "Down by the Old Mill Stream," "Dixie," "Back Home Again in Indiana," etc. This fun was no less real just because it was less spectacular. It simply meant that they had found more than one way of having fun. Some remembered the old days of finding fun in the simple things like popping popcorn, making fudge, pulling taffy, etc.

It must be remembered that the more the variety of enjoyments the more people we can enjoy. When we find fun in many areas, we can enjoy many more people than if we limit ourselves to one area in the search of fun. More important than this, however, is the fact that more people can enjoy you if your fun is varied. People will not have to adapt themselves to you, but you can adapt yourself to them. You can enter into their level of fun and enjoyment and find enjoyment as well as give it. Where is the fun of reading a book, sharing a simple conversation, taking a walk in the park together, or driving around as a family group? "Ah, that is dull," you say. Yes, this is because fun is relative and comparative. This busy, herky-jerky world can only find fun in the fast and furious, the wrong and restless, the big and busy, and in so doing robs itself of many areas of enjoyment. This means that if we find fun only in an isolated area of life, we have to be doing one particular thing to find enjoyment and fun. If we have developed a varied appetite for pleasure, we can find ourselves enjoying just that many different types of experiences and events. To the person who has learned this, whether it be the kids' ballgame on the corner lot, a quiet evening with the family, a Sunday School picnic, a simple conversation with a friend, or a wild time of humor at a party, life affords many more joys, happinesses, pleasures and fun than to the person who has become a specialist finding pleasure in only one area of life.

4. *Remember from past experiences the recipe for fun.* Many times my wife will say while in the home of another lady, "Could I have the recipe for that cake?" The lady has it ready, for she remembers the recipe for successful ventures. The same thing can be applied to life. When a person has a good time, he should make a written list of the ingredients. Hence, he has a recipe for fun and enjoyment that he may do it again and again and again, and even share it with others. Far too many of us have a wonderful experience or a delightful time not realizing the ingredients that made it so. Then the next delightful time will have to be by accident when conditions just happen to be right. If, however, one could sit down at the close of a happy time and list its ingredients, he could "stir" himself a happy time with the proper ingredients, just as he could stir himself a cake like he had before. This is a vital part of developing a capacity for enjoyment.

We must remember that the more we have enjoyed, the less we can enjoy if we are careless. If, for example, life is composed of one hundred enjoyments, then each time we have such an enjoyment we have one less, that is, unless we learn to create enjoyments ourselves. In this way the same pleasure can be enjoyed over and over again. We must not let the acquiring of more mature enjoyments and pleasures keep us from re-experiencing the old ones. Let us not trade one pleasure for another but rather, add one pleasure to another. Keep the ability to enjoy the last pleasure while developing the ability to enjoy the new one or else the cultivating of new enjoyments becomes simply another step in a search for something that cannot be found. How much better it would be if the cultivation of a new enjoyment could simply be the addition of a new dimension to a happiness already found.

5. *The good time of others should always be considered.* As a pastor this is very vital to me. I must always be measuring the enjoyment level of others so as to see to it that they have fun, joy, and satisfaction at various activities. I must not use my humor just to demonstrate that I am the life of the party, but rather I must be unselfish in my humor and think of the enjoyment of another. *Humor is not something to be exhibited, demonstrated, or applauded, but rather it is another of the God-given talents which can be used to make another happy. Used properly and unselfishly it can be a great tool for others. Used carelessly and unwisely it could become a weapon against ourselves.*

Chapter Nineteen

PREACH TO THE BACK ROW

When God called me to preach, all of my talents were hidden. In fact, no one could see them! I could not make a public speech. When I enrolled in college, I took several courses in speech and public speaking the first year. One of the first things I learned was the rule that one should speak to the back row and then the rest of the audience would hear him also. If the person in the back can hear, all the others can hear.

This little rule can become a philosophy of life. If a person will do the smallest task well, the other tasks will take care of themselves. If one can do the least enjoyable chore well, all the others will be done well. If one does well that which is hard for him to do, he will do a good job on the rest. *If one is nice to the ugliest, he will be nice to all. If he is kind to the unkind, then he will of necessity be kind to the kind.*

Anyone can love the lovely, but *he who loves the unlovely will automatically love the lovely.* Anyone can do the easy tasks, but *he that does the hard tasks will subconsciously do the easy tasks.* Anyone can do the challenging job well, but *the one who does well the insignificant work will perform properly the significant task.* Oh, how we need to learn this simple truth: Preach to the back row and everyone else can hear easily.

Someone has well said, "The light that shines the farthest shines the brightest at home." What we are saying is what we have said many times before: The secret to success is not talent, but character; not gifts, but discipline. The successful man must force himself to do that which he is supposed to do though it be an undesirable task. This comes not from inspiration from without, but from within. It comes from our doing the task because we are supposed to do it, not because we are inspired to do it. It comes from obedience to schedule, obedience to planning, and obedience to discipline. Basically, it is obedience to self — when self is disciplined. It is obedience to duty, obedience to right, and a subconscious doing of that which is supposed to be done. This is character.

Chapter Twenty

DANGERS OF SUCCESS

Someone has said that what a man is can be determined by what it takes to stop him. In a sense this is true. The greatest test in life, however, to this author is not how he takes the tough places in life, but how he learns to take the successes in life. Many people have stood the tests, trials, and heartaches that have confronted them but could not stand prosperity or success. Many institutions, churches, and nations have withstood the dark hours but could not stand the prosperous ones.

In this brief article we will not attempt to list all of the dangers of success, but we will enumerate some.

1. *Self pride.* It is very interesting to note that God uses only small people, small things, and small churches. This does not mean that the small cannot become big. One does not have to read far in the Bible to find that the way up is down, the way to be the greatest is to be the servant of all, and the way to become big is to become small. It was said of Saul that God could use him when he was little in his own eyes. Someone has said, "Immorality has slain its thousands; pride, its tens of thousands." Certainly this is true. Let us always realize that whatever we are, whatever we have done, and whatever we have is all because of the grace of God. There is nothing good about any of us except Jesus Christ. Let us never forget it.

2. *Self-confidence.* When the days of testing are over and we have thrown ourselves upon God for His strength and help, then ofttimes come the days of success and victory. It is then when we often feel that we have no need of God, and it is then when we really need Him the most. Actually the tough times are caused by opposition from without. In prosperity our opposition comes from within, and this is the most dangerous of all. Many a Christian has withstood the onslaught and attacks of the Devil on all sides only to find himself defeated by self-confidence because of his past victories. He looks about him and finds that all of his enemies are slain. What he does not

know is that inside of him the enemy of self-confidence is lurking for the deadly blow.

3. *Self-satisfaction.* The Holy Spirit led the inspired writer to say, "Where there is no vision the people perish." It is easy for us to arrive at a certain plateau of victory that causes us to lose our vision for the future. It was Alexander the Great who said, "I have no more worlds to conquer." This was said at the tender age of 29 and led to his downfall. The Christian should always be setting new goals, looking for new heights, and pointing to new victories. We should never look back and gloat; we should look forward and dream and plan. Let us never be self-satisfied until we awake in His likeness.

4. *Selfishness.* Success often brings this enemy to the forefront. Perhaps God gives us a great victory and much success. Then the Devil tells us that we were the cause for the victory. We are tempted to forget others who helped us and stood by us on the road to success. No man lives unto himself or dies unto himself, and there are no self-made men. The Apostle Paul said that he could but speak the things which he had seen and heard. We are certainly influenced by our environment and those with whom we work. We should readily give the major share of the credit to those who help us, lest the deadly enemy of selfishness creep up from within to defeat us, not in hours of trial, but in hours of triumph.

5. *Self-evaluation.* When we have been through the battles, won the victories, and have found ourselves successful, then we often begin to measure our degree of success. This is a crucial time in our lives for this is the time we want to evaluate ourselves, but we should not. There was not time to pause in the battle to find our positions for the standings are decided when the game is over. Let us not evaluate ourselves by growth, size, building, etc., but rather let us keep pressing on realizing the work is the important thing, not the status which we have achieved or the plateau to which we have arrived.

6. *Self-analysis.* There are certain tried and tested means by which success is gained. Often when success comes, we begin using new methods. A businessman who works his way to the top is tempted not to work as hard to keep successful as he did to get successful. We should remember that the same thing that

gets us there keeps us there. The same diligence, the same humility, the same spirit, the same character, the same integrity, the same honesty, the same earnestness — these and other characteristics that brought about our success are the characteristics that will sustain our success.

How easy it is for us to win the battle of Jericho and lose the battle of Ai. How easy it is to fight and defeat the wild beast and be destroyed by the little foxes. Certainly, what we are is shown in the heat of the battle, but *many people who have won the battle have lost the victory. Many a runner who won the race stumbled at the Bema and broke a leg while receiving his crown.*

Chapter Twenty-One

THE HORSE AND THE MULE
(The Need for Leadership)

"Be ye not as the horse, or as the mule, which have no understanding: whose mouth must be held in with bit and bridle, lest they come near unto thee." —Psalms 32:9.

Dr. Lee Roberson has said, "Everything rises and falls on leadership." One of the great needs in our generation is the need for leaders. Everyone to some extent is a leader. The pastor in the church, the teacher in the class, the superintendent in the department, the father in the home, the mother and the children all have a sphere of leadership. The great problem of being a leader is that of having to start the fire yourself. Many people can serve God and become a blessing once they have blessed by another, but someone has to begin the service. Someone has to have a blessing before the service starts. He must find his blessing alone so that he in turn can lead others to be blessed. How to do this is the subject now presented for our thinking.

1. *The leader must have inner motivation.* I have known many preachers who could preach a great message if it were preceded by someone else's message. I have known many singers who could sing a great solo if they could be inspired first. The leader, however, must have inner motivation. His motivation must come from character and not from inspiration. One who depends upon external inspiration becomes unpredictable because he is giving himself to powers outside his own control as he has no power over external motivation. One who through character and duty has learned to gain his inspiration from within will develop more consistency and hence, better leadership ability.

One should learn things that inspire him. I once heard a great preacher say, "I am always looking for things that inspire me." This is very important. When one knows what inspires him he should write it down. In fact a list of such things should be made in order that we may learn how to be inspired from within rather than from without.

2. *The leader must have predictability.* A follower can shout today and cry tomorrow but a leader must offer predictability to his followers. They must learn what to expect from him. To be sure, a leader will have high hours and low hours, but he must learn to conceal his disappointments and heartaches and walk predictably before his followers. This means that a leader will have to walk on the highest level he is able to maintain. It is better to go 60 miles an hour all of the time than 90, then 10, then 80, then 100, and then 20. Such leadership does not prompt mature followship.

3. *The leader must be able to fill the appetite he creates in followers.* In other words, the leader's production must be able to fill his image. He must not lead the followers to more than he can give and he must not create appetites in the followers that he cannot fill.

Many preachers err in this respect by announcing flashy titles that create in the minds of their people appetites for something that the talent, knowledge, and ability of the leader cannot fill.

4. *A leader should have a checklist.* He must never trust his memory. There is no one to remind the leader what to do. In every obligation he should have a list before him as his reminder.

5. *The leader must know where he is going.* He must also sell the follower on the fact that he knows where he is going. The leader must look down the road and plan the trip. He should plan on the trip several points of fulfillment and arrival. For example, when our family takes a vacation, I draw up a schedule. I want to arrive in this town at this time and at the next town at a certain time, etc. On a 1000-mile trip one can have twenty goals to reach and hence feel a sense of fulfillment twenty times. Whereas another would simply have the 1000-mile goal as the only goal and only feel one sense of fulfillment. The leader must remind the people of intermediate goals as well as the ultimate goal. Consequently, the followers (and the leader too, for that matter) can keep a sense of achievement as they reach little goals on the way to

the big goal.

A good illustration of this is a football game. The ultimate goal is to win the championship. There is a more immediate goal of winning the present game. Then there is still a smaller goal of making a touchdown; however, the most immediate appetite to satisfy is that of making a first down. The stands cheer some over a first down, more over a touchdown, still more over victory, and most over the championship. One's life should be this way and the leader should plan the activities of his followers so as to satisfy secondary appetites as well as the primary one. There must be first downs in life as well as touchdowns. This is why it is often more satisfying to make a touchdown by a series of first downs than to score on a long play. The long play may be more immediately satisfying and exciting. This is why life's victories are won bascially on a series of first downs. People who take the short cuts seldom win the final victory.

6. *The leader should also be a good follower.* Every leader also has a sphere of life in which he follows. The corporal leads the privates but follows the sergeant. The sergeant leads the corporals but follows the lieutenant. The lieutenant leads the sergeants but follows the captain. The captain leads the lieutenant but follows the major. The major leads the captain but follows the colonel. The colonel leads the major but follows the general, etc.

The Sunday School teacher leads the class but follows the superintendent. The superintendent leads the teacher but follows the pastor. To expect followship for his leadership, the leader must present followship to his leadership. If I expect my followers to follow me, then I must follow those who lead me. Then whom is the general to follow? He is to follow the Heavenly Father. Here each of us becomes a follower. The writers have said, "Where Ever He Leads I'll Go," "Where He Leads Me I Will Follow," "Have Thine Own Way, Lord, Have Thine Own Way," "All the Way My Saviour Leads Me," and "He Leadeth Me, O Blessed Thought, O Paths with Heavenly Comfort Wrought." To be a successful leader, one must be a successful follower.

7. *It is wise for the leader to identify himself with the*

followers. When Ezekiel was going to preach to the Jews in captivity he said, "I sat where they sat." In other words, he went to the seat of the follower and sat there. Having learned the heart and the feeling of the follower, he now is a more capable leader. One of the things that I have done for years in my church is to go through a little mental calisthenics when I walk out on the platform. I try to look at the people and feel what they feel. For a moment I sit in their seats. This is expecially true in a funeral service. The leader must feel the heartbeat of the follower and must know what it is to sit where he sits.

8. *A leader should list the times and means of success.* There is a reason for success. It comes as a direct result of the proper ingredients. When a leader (or anyone for that matter) succeeds, he should immediately write down the formula that he used. This would even apply to followers. When a follower pleases his superior, he should write down the ingredients used so as to use them again and again.

9. *The leader must spend much time with the Saviour.* I will never forget the day in my life when I realized that I would never have a pastor again. For nearly a quarter of a century I have had no pastor. Hence, I have had to spend much time with the Lord. No one can be a successful leader who does not walk with God. Since there is followship in each of us and a need for security in the strongest of us, the one who has few or no earthly leaders must know intimately the One Who is the Leader of us all.

Oftentimes young preachers ask me what advice would supersede every other advice that I would give to a young preacher. Immediately I answer, "Walk with God."

Chapter Twenty-Two

MEEKNESS

"Blessed are the meek: for they shall inherit the earth."
(Matthew 5:5)

"But let it be the hidden man of the heart, in that which is
not corruptible, even the ornament of a meek and quiet spirit,
which is in the sight of God of great price." (1 Peter 3:4)

"But thou, O man of God, flee these things; and follow after
righteousness, godliness, faith, love, patience, meekness." I
Timothy 6:11)

"Brethren, if a man be overtaken in a fault, ye which are
spiritual, restore such an one in the spirit of meekness;
considering thyself, lest thou also be tempted." (Galatians 6:1)

"To speak evil of no man, to be no brawlers, but gentle,
shewing all meekness unto all men." (Titus 3:2)

The word "meekness" in the Bible comes from the word
"mecca" which means level. It does not mean, as some would
think, that one looks up to everyone else and thinks of himself
as being inferior. Meekness is not fright, neither is it possessing
an inferiority complex, but rather it is looking to everyone
from a level position. Meekness looks up to no one and down to
no one. Meekness does not look up to the rich, nor down to the
poor; up to the educated, nor down to the uneducated; up to
the higher ranks, nor down to the lower rank.

Of course, *I do not know who the best Christian in the world*
is, but whoever he is, he does not know it. In fact, he does not
think of himself at all. His greatness is lost in obedience to his
Saviour. I do not know who the biggest preacher in the world is,
but whoever he is, he does not know it. I do not know who the
greatest person in the world is, but whoever he is, he has not
found out about it yet. It has been my joy to meet some of the
great Christians of our generation and to fellowship with some
of the greatest servants of God living today. I have noticed in
every case that these men do not feel either inferior or superior.

This does not mean, however, that we are not to respect
authority. We certainly ought to respect the position of our

superiors, but we are not to idolize their person. Romans 13 tells us that we are to respect the authority of rulers. Ephesians 6:1 reminds us that we are to respect the authority of our parents. Ephesians 6:5 tells us that we are to respect the authority of our employers. Certainly we are to respect the authority of age and the position of the pastor. We are to give respect to those who have had more success than we, those with more experiences than we, and those who teach us or have taught us.

I can recall my mother teaching me about the subject of meekness when I was a little boy. She told me never to look up to anyone or down to anyone. She taught me to respect the position of my superiors and of those in authority over me, but she reminded me that though I was a poor boy, I should look everyone straight in the eye. What a tremendous truth this is and how necessary it is to the molding of the character of our youth.

Chapter Twenty-Three

PREPAREDNESS OR PERPLEXITIES

When I was a kid about eleven years of age, I started taking long walks and thinking about life. One of the thoughts that occupied my mind the most was the fact that most of life's perplexities are caused by being caught off guard. It seemed to me then, and it seems to me now, that the right kind of person prepares himself for life's changes and transitions.

As I look back over my life, I find that the two most perplexing times were those for which I was unprepared. The first of these was the death of my father. I was not prepared for it. I had not even thought about it, and because of this, there was a great adjustment I had to make.

The second of these perplexing times was my leaving Garland, Texas, to move to Hammond, Indiana. I thought I was in Garland for a lifetime. I had no desire or intention of leaving when suddenly God called me away. It took eighteen months for me to get over the shock of this heartbreak simply because I had not prepared for such a move. Much of our mental illness and many of our nervous breakdowns are caused by the fact that we take life as it comes, never preparing for its inevitables. We find ourselves in frustration and perplexity because of the lack of preparedness.

1. *Prepare for an era.* Life changes. Eras of life come and go. This is true for school, church, an individual, a home, or any organization or institution. We must prepare ourselves for the inevitable changes which take place during the transition from one era to another.

For example, when we built our present auditorium, I had regular meetings with my staff reminding them of the possible pitfalls of entering into a new auditorium. The song leader must remember that voices do not carry as well in a big building. People cannot see the song leader as easily in a larger building. The numbers must be announced more distinctly in a bigger building. These are just a few of the many things that must be considered. Many churches have lost their joy and spirit because they were not prepared for such a move.

82

In my own ministry I have realized the changes that must come as one era goes and another era comes. I started preaching when I was nineteen years of age. For a long time I was a youthful pastor. As I grow older I find I must discard some of the older mannerisms and add some new ones. I must give constant thought concerning my attire, my vocabulary, my manners, etc. I must prepare myself to be a middle-aged preacher. Then someday I must prepare myself to be an older preacher. Many preachers, because of a lack of such preparation, find themselves frustrated in their ministry. This same thing is true in the life of a layman. We must always be foreseeing new eras in life and preparing for them.

2. *Prepare for changes in relationships.* Relationships in life undergo changes. If you are a parent, you have already noticed that the relationships with your children change. The child is constantly changing in his behavior toward his parents. This is God's way of preparing the child for going out on his own. From infancy to adulthood there is a gradual withdrawing from Mother and Father. Of course, this should not mature or ripen too early, but proper preparation will avoid heartbreak.

I can recall as a teen-age boy how I began to realize that I was going to have to leave my mother and go into the army. World War II was on at that time. I can recall gradually withdrawing myself from mother and unraveling my life from around hers in order to avoid the heartbreak that would come if I failed to do so.

At this writing my daughter Becky has only one more year in high school. I have begun to prepare myself for this transition. No father ever hated to see his daughter leave home any more than I, but I must realize the inevitables of life and substitute preparedness for perplexity. I must realize the happiness that lies ahead in this phase of my life. I must magnify the benefits and minimize the liabilities. This will enable me to enjoy the new phase of my relationship with my daughter rather than lament its drawbacks.

Many people live in a utopian tomorrow while others dream of a happy yesterday. I want to live in a happy utopia today! Hence, I must watch others and learn from them. I must foresee the changes and transitions of life in order to prepare myself for them and receive the fullest from them.

Much is said in this book about the friend relationship. It never changes. There need be no preparation for transition periods. The needs of the friend relationship are always the same, and though the relationship may deepen, it need never enter into a new era that will cause perplexity if there is not preparedness. One can nestle back in a friend relationship and comfortably relax in it, developing it to its deepest depths within the bounds of right realizing that it is a bond that need never be broken and a tie that need never be severed.

Each of us must choose whether our future will be described by preparedness or perplexity. *If we prepare ourselves for life's inevitables, we will not be perplexed by life's transitions.*

Chapter Twenty-Four

THE BODY

Nothing happens accidentally. Discipline and character always accompany success. The same is true with physical strength and health. One does not have a strong body accidentally. To be sure, some are more gifted than others in this respect, but many strong and healthy people have dissipated their bodies, whereas many people with care and discipline have caused their bodies to outlast their expected usefulness. Remember that one serves the Lord with his body. When health is gone, usefulness is gone. When our bodies are no longer able to convey thoughts, then we will be of no value to God or to others. Several simple rules will help you to have a stronger body.

1. *Let God have your body.* *"I beseech you therefore, brethren, by the mercies of God, that ye present your bodies a living sacrifice, holy, acceptable unto God, which is your reasonable service." (Romans 12:1)* I was not a big boy as a child. I did not have an extremely healthy body. I did, however, take my hands and say, "God, they are Yours." I took my feet and said, "God, they are Yours." I touched my eyes and said, "God, they are Yours." I did the same thing with each member of my body. It is amazing what God can do with a little bit.

2. *Dedicate your body as a temple.* *"Flee fornication. Every sin that a man doeth is without the body; but he that committeth fornication sinneth against his own body. What? know ye not that your body is the temple of the Holy Ghost which is in you, which ye have of God, and ye are not your own?" (I Corinthians 6:18, 19)* This teaches us that the body is the temple of the Holy Spirit. We should take the same care of the body today that the Jews did of the temple in the Old Testament. The Bible seems to imply that the body sins are the worst sins. Could this be because the body is the temple of the Holy Spirit? Our bodies should be as dedicated to God and His service as were the furnishings of the Old Testament temple.

3. *Keep your body clean.* Since the body is the temple of the Holy Spirit, it should be kept clean both outwardly and

85

inwardly. Regular baths should be taken. Proper deodorant should be used. Men should shave carefully. The hair should have regular care. The teeth should be kept clean. Nothing was kept more immaculately clean than the Old Testament temple. Since the body is the temple of the New Testament, it should be likewise clean. Certainly this should apply to morals. Adultery, necking, petting, and promiscuous behaving between the sexes should certainly be out as far as God's people are concerned. Keep the body clean. There is something about a clean body that God can use.

5. *Keep your body straight.* It is very important that a Christian should learn how to walk properly and sit properly.No Christian should be slouchy. In our family altar we have taught our children such habits. We have had our girls to practice walking across the room. We have taught them to walk like girls and sit like girls. We have taught our boy to walk with a manly walk and sit with a manly posture. Keep the body straight. It is God's. Let it be a good testimony.

6. *Keep your body coordinated.* This is of vital importance. A person should know how to handle his body with dexterity and coordination. At this writing I am 41 years of age. I have played sports all of my life. I have kept my body in fairly good condition, and because of this, I was able to save my sister's life. She and I were crossing a street in South Bend, Indiana, where I was preaching in a Bible Conference. A car turned left, not seeing us. I saw the car and jumped back. My sister did not see it. The car was about to hit her when I almost subconsciously grabbed her and pulled her from the path of the car. It barely scraped her and knocked her to the cement, but tests for injuries proved negative. She would p r o b a b l y not be alive today were it not for my coordination.

My coordination also saved my own life once. In World War II, I joined the Paratroopers. On my fifth jump the parachute did not open. I was one second from the ground when I quickly pulled my reserve chute. It opened and saved my life. Certainly a man with manly coordination can reach more men for Christ. For both men and women coordination should be a must for the body.

7. *Keep the body properly fed.* Remember, food is fuel. It

is tragic that we feed our dogs better fuel than we feed our own bodies. We carefully choose the food for our pigs, horses, and cows, and then gulp down most anything for self. Proper vitamins, Bible foods, and Bible stimulants should be taken by the Christian. The Christian, of course, should not be guilty of drinking liquor, smoking, etc. I have found it helpful not even to use coffee or carbonated drinks.Why not try honey or orange juice for a stimulant?

It is also wise for a Christian to fast occasionally. Occasional fasting is certainly physicially helpful to the body. Sometimes a Christian should pray and fast.

Many times I have been preaching and found myself developing a bit of voice trouble. When such times occur, a juice fast often is the answer. Much throat trouble is caused by the stomach. To say the least, a Christian should put the proper fuel in his body so that he may use it to the glory of God.

8. *Keep the body rested.* It is important that the body receive the proper amount of rest. This rest should be done at regular hours if possible. Much of what is commonly called "fellowship" by preachers should be sacrificed for rest and work. I have found it wise to avoid late-hour snacks as well as late, heavy thinking. Sometimes a few exercises before going to bed are good to relax the body and make it rest better. Certainly we should not develop the habits of sluggards. Yet we should realize that the body is the Lord's and needs to be rested regularly.

9. *Keep the body under subjection.* Appetites are good servants but not good masters. No appetite should control the body. Let the Christian always yield his body to Christ and be master over his own appetites.

10. *Keep the body strong.* Exercise is very important to the body. I find that I can do more work when I do regular calisthenics and exercise. I find it is good to run some as well as to do calisthenics. Now there are as many suggestions for this as there are people, but I find if I run a mile or so a day and do about fifteen minutes of heavy calisthenics, my lungs are in better condition for preaching, and I have a healthier body to use for the glory of God.

With proper dedication of the body, proper cleanliness,

neatness, coordination, food, rest, exercise, and control, one can live longer to the glory of God.

Chapter Twenty-Five

DANGEROUS AND IMPORTANT TIMES
FOR STAYING IN THE WILL OF GOD

It is always important to stay in God's will. However, at certain times of life, it becomes even more difficult than usual. Some of these times are listed here:

1. *The obeying of parents during childhood.* It is important for young people to remember that their parents represent God. As children obey parents now they will obey God later. This is why it is very important that parents insist that their children obey and that proper punishment be given for disobedience. Occasionally a parent will say, "I love my child too much to discipline him." The truth is simply this: If a parent loves a child, he will spank him and discipline him. A child simply MUST be taught to obey his parents. If he gets out of the will of God here, he will no doubt be out of the will of God for the rest of his life.

2. *In choosing a high school.* It is very interesting to find out how many people marry their high school sweethearts. Once while preaching along these lines, I asked those who married someone they met for the first time in high school to raise their hands. It was very shocking and revealing, for a large percentage lifted their hands. Hence, if there is a choice in the choosing of a high school, it is of vital importance that the proper choice be made.

3. *The centering of a young person's life.* Of course, Christian young people should be good students in school, and pastors and Sunday School workers should encourage them to be so. It is usually wise, however, for young people to be very careful about extracurricular school activities. The use of spare time should be centered around the church and the church activities. Because of this, the church should provide activities for the young people. Young people choose mates from those whom they know best, and most of these mates are chosen from people met at the extracurricular activities

where the most time is spent. A Christian young person has a far better chance to marry another Christian young person if his spare time is spent in church activities. They are also more likely to go to a good Christian college because they are spending their lives with those who are going to attend Christian colleges. It is very important that a young person center his life around the work of Jesus Christ and the New Testament Church.

4. *The choosing or accepting of a date.* In a public service I asked for the married folks to raise their hands who had no idea on their first date that they wanted to marry the person who later became their mate. This response was also revealing.

It seems like a small thing for a girl to say "yes" or "no" to a boy who asks for a date. However, no girl should have a date with a boy unless she feels that he would make a good Christian husband. Likewise, no boy should ask a girl for a date unless he feels she would make a good Christian wife. It is wise for young people not to date someone whom they feel would not make a proper mate. One never knows when admiration shall turn to love.

5. *The choosing of a job or vocation.* Here is one of the easiest times for a person to leave the will of God. Several good rules for choosing a job or vocation are as follows:

a. *Choose one which is beneficial to mankind.* I advise young people not to choose jobs such as professional sports, acting, etc. These activities were meant to be recreation, not vocation. A job does not have to be a well-paying job or a glamorous job. Some helpful jobs which could be chosen are collecting garbage, building houses, being a plumber, being an electrician, or any one of hundreds of vocations beneficial to one's fellow man.

b. *It is usually best to choose a basic job.* For example, a young man came to me trying to decide whether to go into the grocery business or the boat making business. I showed him that in case of depression or recession, the grocery business would still be in demand, whereas the boat business would be extinct. It is always wise to consider what economic changes would do to one's job.

c. *The vocation should be honest and right.* Such things as selling liquor or entering into any other wicked vocation should not even be considered.

d. *One should not commit himself to a company.* These are days of chain stores and monopolies. It is certainly not wrong for a person to work for a nationwide chain. It is wrong for that person to commit himself to move wherever his company wants to move him. This takes God's will out of it and makes it the will of the company. Of course, this is wrong!

e. *One should always consider the availability of good fundamental churches near his place of work.* It is spiritual suicide for one's children when he carelessly takes a job in an area not knowing if there is a good fundamental church available. There is a man in my present pastorate whose company is moving. He has a very responsible position with his company. Rather than leave and take his boys out of our church, he is leaving the company with which he has been for many years and is staying in Hammond. We think he is making the right decision.

f. *Do not move because the company transfers you.* Suppose your pastor got up in the pulpit next Sunday and said, "I am changing churches because I have been offered more money." You would be completely shocked and overwhelmed, but he has just as much right to do this as you. No person has a right to take a job because it offers more money or a promotion. The only thing that a Christian has a right to do is the will of God.

Let each Christian pray and seek God's guidance as he seeks his vocation for life.

5. *The choosing of a church.* "Attend the church of your choice," and "Go to church in your own neighborhood" are two of many fallacious statements being made nowadays concerning church attendance. All churches are *not* alike! All churches do not preach and believe the Bible. It is very vital that a person choose a church that believes in the verbal inspiration of the Scriptures, the deity of Jesus Christ, and salvation by grace through faith. It is also wise to place one's life and membership in a church that is actively evangelistic and offers a strong program for the entire family. When a family

chooses a church, oftentimes the mates for their children, the colleges their children will attend, as well as scores of other things are being chosen at the same time.

6. *The purchasing of a house.* God's will is also very important when the buying of a house is being considered. Certainly care should be taken and prayer should be offered in the making of such a decision.

It must be remembered that the will of God is the greatest thing one can do in life. There is no greater accomplishment than to be in the will of God. There is no greater joy than to be in the will of God. There is no greater safety than to be in the will of God. Let us always stay in His will and take extra care when life-changing decisions must be made.

Chapter Twenty-Six

WORK

Someone has well said, "I believe in luck. The harder I work the luckier I get." The secret to any success is hard work. Whether it is the building of a church or a hot-dog stand, the making of a good life or good grades, work is the great secret to success. No amount of talent can take its place. No gifts can substitute for it. Even if per chance one could obtain success without work, it would fail to satisfy. The Bible has much to say about work, and we should look at a few of its passages.

1. *Work is spiritual.* *"The soul of the sluggard desireth, and hath nothing: but the soul of the diligent shall be made fat." (Proverbs 13:4)* One of the great mistakes of our generation is dividing the sacred from the secular. As somone has said, "To the Christian every day is a holy day; every bush is a burning bush; and every place is a sacred place." Being a good Christian is not having a good feeling, having a good cry, or making a good speech, but it is obeying the commands of God and doing His work. One can learn all the lingo, attend all the meetings, ride the spiritual merry-go-rounds, give a glowing testimony, and still not be a good Christian. The great test of Christianity is obedience. Jesus said, *"Ye are my friends, if ye do whatsoever I command you." (John 15:14)* He also said, *"If you love Me, keep My commandments." (John 14:15)* Work is spiritual!

2. *Work is succeeding.* The word "work" implies to produce or achieve. The salesman gets no commission for trying to sell. He gets a commission for selling. This means that when we do a job, we áre to do it well and point to success.

The question then comes, "How can I succeed?" The first Psalm will answer that question: *"Blessed is the man that walketh not in the counsel of the ungodly, nor standeth in the way of sinners, nor sitteth in the seat of the scornful. But his delight is in the law of the Lord; and in His law doth he meditate day and night. And he shall be like a tree planted by the rivers of water, that bringeth forth his fruit in his season; his leaf also shall not wither; and whatsoever he doeth shall prosper. The ungodly are not so: but are like the chaff which*

93

the wind driveth away. Therefore the ungodly shall not stand in the judgment, nor sinners in the congregation of the righteous. For the Lord knoweth the way of the righteous: but the way of the ungodly shall perish. " Notice also Joshua 1:1-8. *"Now after the death of Moses the servant of the Lord it came to pass, that the Lord spake unto Joshua the son of Nun, Moses' minister, saying, Moses my servant is dead; now therefore arise, go over this Jordan, thou, and all this people, unto the land which I do give to them, even to the children of Israel. Every place that the sole of your foot shall tread upon, that have I given unto you, as I said unto Moses. From the wilderness and this Lebanon even unto the great river, the river Euphrates, all the land of the Hittites, and unto the great sea toward the going down of the sun, shall be your coast. There shall not any man be able to stand before thee all the days of thy life: as I was with Moses, so I will be with thee: I will not fail thee, nor forsake thee. Be strong and of a good courage: for unto this people shalt thou divide for an inheritance the land, which I sware unto their fathers to give them. Only be thou strong and very courageous, that thou mayest observe to do according to all the law, which Moses my servant commanded thee: turn not from it to the right hand or to the left, that thou mayest propser whithersoever thou goest. This book of the law shall not depart out of thy mouth; but thou shalt meditate therein day and night, that thou mayest observe to do according to all that is written therein: for then thou shalt make thy way prosperous. and then thou shalt have good success.*"In these verses we find a guaranteed recipe for success. This is a plan that will not fail.

From childhood one should be taught that if a job is worth doing, it is worth doing well. Every job should be done thoroughly and carefully. When your children are growing up and have a task to do, let them carry the task through to completion. They will learn character, and you will gain a helper. This is a very vital part of rearing a child.

3. *The worker should do what needs to be done. "And, lo, it was all grown over with thorns, and nettles had covered the face thereof, and the stone wall thereof was broken down."* (*Proverbs 24:31*). No task is too little to demand our best, and no task is too great but what our best plus God is enough.

4. *If a person does not work, he should not eat.* "*For even when we were with you, this we commanded you, that if any would not work, neither should he eat.*" *(II Thessalonians 3:10)* College-age students who are not studying should not be supported by parents at home. Socialists and Communists who refuse to work are not supposed to eat. No poverty program, whether by church or state, should feed people who refuse to work. We do not help a lazy fellow when we feed him. Rather we help him when we teach him that if he does not work, he does not eat. This is God's plan. Liberal Bible rejectors try to make their own social standards and develop their own social programs, but the Bible still speaks that if a man will not work, he shall not eat.

5. *One should learn to work without a boss.* "*Which having no guide, overseer, or ruler.*" *(Proverbs 6:7)* Nothing quite reveals the lack of character in a person more than for him to refuse to work when the boss is not looking. The simple truth is that a little ant has more character than a lot of people. The sluggard should go to the ant bed and look down at the little red insect, salute him, and envy him because he has more character. A person has reached a very sad state when an ant on an ant hill has more character than he. We should work for work's sake, for integrity's sake, for honesty's sake, and for decency's sake.

One of the great problems of our generation is mass production and big-city factories. It often eliminates one's pride in his work and takes away trades, skills, etc. In spite of this, however, one should develop such character that he will do his work simply because he is supposed to do his work. Diligence and discipline should compel us to do our best at every task.

In the training of a child he should be given definite duties. These duties should be outlined carefully so that both child and parent understand. Then the child should be taught what he is to do and how to do it. He should be taught the willingness to serve. He should not be paid for his duty unless his job is done well. The parent should not do the job for the child after he has failed, but rather, the parent should make him do it again and make him do it well.

Work is spiritual. One cannot be a good Christian and not work. One cannot be a good Christian and not obey. One cannot be a good Christian and not do his best at every task.

Chapter Twenty-Seven

SO YOU ARE OUT OF GOD'S WILL

"There came then His brethren and His mother, and, standing without, sent unto Him, calling Him." (Mark 3:31)
"Jesus saith unto them, My meat is to do the will of Him that sent Me, and to finish His work." (John 4:34)

Most Christians at one time or another find themselves at least a bit out of the will of God. As someone has said, "It is not a sin for a bird to land on your head, but it is a sin for you to allow him to build a nest there." It is easy to get out of the will of God. It is hard to get back in the will of God. The following thoughts are given to those who have slipped out of God's will:

1. *If the door is still open, go back through it.* If a pastor has left a church and he should not have left, and if the church is still pastorless, he may go back. If the job is still open, the one who left may return. If one has gone to the wrong school, he may go to the right school. If one has entered the wrong profession, he may rectify that by entering the right profession. If one is engaged to the wrong girl or boy, he can break the engagement. In other words, if one does not perform wrong by doing so, he should re-enter the door through which he left the will of God.

2. *Go back the way you came.* If one left the will of God when he quit paying his debts, he should get back in the will of God by paying the debts. If one left the will of God by hurting people, he should get back in the will of God by making reconciliation. Undo what has been done if it is at all possible, and go back to the will of God where you came out of His will.

3. *Never do wrong to get back in the will of God.* Suppose, for example, the pastor leaves a church that he should not have left. The church then calls a new pastor. In such a case, the former pastor has forfeited the will of God and should in no way attempt to regain the church. Suppose someone marries the wrong person. If the one he should have married is already married, it would be wrong to break up that home in order to

get the person that God had for him in the first place. Never do wrong in getting back into the will of God. Two wrongs do not make a right!

4. *Seek the acceptable will of God.* Many people find themselves so far out of God's perfect will that they can never get back in it. If the wrong person has been married, for example, then there is no way to get back rightly in the will of God concerning one's marriage. God will allow one to live with his present mate in His acceptable will under such conditions. This same is true about one who has committed some sin that would cause him to forfeit the perfect will of God. Here is a man whom God has called to preach, but the involvements of his life have made it impossible for him to do so. Perhaps he has complicated his life so much that it would be unscriptural for him to be a pastor. This means he has forever sacrificed the perfect will of God, but he can go ahead by teaching a Sunday School class, winning souls, etc. in the acceptable will of God and be a very fruitful Christian.

5. *Get close to someone in the perfect will of God.* This is very important. If a person's life has caused him to forfeit the perfect will of God, he may then be in the acceptable will of God, but perhaps he could accomplish more by working with someone in the perfect will of God and being a part of that someone's ministry.

6. *Work harder.* As mentioned in another chapter, work is the secret to success. If one finds himself unable to get back into the perfect will of God, he may find the acceptable will of God for his life, and by working harder than those in the perfect will of God, he may certainly do much to make amends. He may even get as much done as the person in the perfect will of God. If for any reason you have forfeited the perfect will of God for your life, work that much harder to make up for the mistake and try to accomplish as much in life as possible.

All of us know about the athlete who is not as gifted with as many natural gifts as others, and yet accomplishes more. He is not the natural athelete; he is a scrambler. By hustle, practice, and hard work he oftentimes surpasses the more gifted one. This is also true in God's service.

7. *Use your testimony to warn others.* If you have left the

perfect will of God, admit it to help others avoid making the same mistakes. Especially should you be a help to children and young people.

8. *Be sure you do not blame the cause.* In some cases one's mate may be associated with his leaving the perfect will of God. He should in no case blame his mate. This simply adds fuel to the fire and insult to the injury.

9. *Do not lament, but be thankful.* Take your medicine like a good boy and be thankful that a least something has been reclaimed and salvaged in life.

So you are out of the will of God. I am sorry. If possible, go about getting back into the perfect will of God immediately. If this is impossible, get right with God, have your life reclaimed for His service, and do His acceptable will. God can still use you. Let Him do so.

Chapter Twenty-Eight

FAITHFULNESS

The word "faithful" in the Bible comes from a word which means "to be trusted" or "to be reliable." It is a twin to the word "believe" as concerning believing upon Christ for salvation.

Faithfulness does not mean "not being unfaithful." Suppose a wife says that she is faithful to her husband. She may mean that she is not guilty of negative acts against her husband. On the other hand, she may not be doing anything positive for him. *Faithfulness is not the absence of the negative, but the presence of the positive.* For example, a person who does not come to church is unfaithful. He cannot excuse himself by saying he has not been to another church.

We should discipline ourselves to be faithful to many things. Some of these are listed below:

1. Duties and tasks. One should discipline himself to do what he is supposed to do. It is vitally important that one's task becomes his employer. It is important that we get up at the same time every day. This is especially true in the case of people whose employment and duties do not consist of punching a time clock. A salesman, a pastor, and other such people can be successful only as they discipline themselves to be faithful to their duties and tasks. Whatever one has to do he should do and do it well. He should designate a time to do it and then do it at that time.

2. Punctuality. In the building of character, one must learn to be punctual. This means he should be faithful to his appointmenst. He should not develop the habit of always being late. He must be dependable. This is one reason, at the First Baptist Church of Hammond, we start our services on time. We do not start one minute late, but rather, exactly on time. If 600 people wait one minute, 600 minutes are lost, or 10 working hours. If 2,400 people wait one minute an entire work week is lost as far as time is concerned. We have all heard it said about someone, "You can set your clock by him." This means that he is at least in one respect a man of

100

character. How important this is.

3. Church. It is important that a child be taught to be faithful to his church. There are several reasons for this. Life's principles are being set. One of these principles should be faithfulness to the house of God. Many years ago I decided that I would go to church every Sunday morning, every Sunday night, and every Wednesday night. This has been my policy through the years. There have been a few times when I was ill, but unless I was very ill, I have been to the house of God and have been there faithfully. This cannot be overly stressed.

You recall what Thomas missed by being absent the first time the apostles met with the risen Christ. You remember his doubting spirit. There are many doubting, cantankerous Christians who would not be so had they been faithful to God's house.

One will do later what he does now. It is a good idea now to start the habit of faithfulness to the house of God. The sermon you need the most may be preached the service you are not present, and it may never be repeated.

4. Spiritual habits. I find it possible for a person to read the Bible all the time and not be a good Christian, to pray all the time and not be a good Christian, and even to win souls all the time and not be a good Christian. It is wise for a person to set a schedule for spiritual habits—a set time to pray, a set time to study the Bible, a set time to go soul winning. One should be faithful to these times and obedient to his schedule, and at the same time, keep a balanced Christian life. It is a good idea to sit down and list all the things that the Christian is supposed to do. Then find time in the schedule for them, and observe the schedule with all diligence and faithfulness.

5. Principles. Our loyalties should be to principles and not to institutions. Far too many of us have pledged our faithfulness and loyalty to denominations, churches, schools, etc. They change so gradually that we do not notice it; therefore, we change with them. The day comes when both institution and Christian have changed and neither realizes it. The landmark has been moved so gradually that, as is the case with the hands on the clock, it was not noticed. This is the reason we should be faithful to principles. When the institution goes outside our principles, we should hold the principles and discard the institution unless we can bring it back in proper focus with right principles.

For example, I have taught my boy, David, to protect his sisters. A few years ago I saw him beating up on a little kid. I had told him not to fight. I went over, jerked him off the kid, and said, "What are you doing?"

He looked at me and said, "He called my sister a dirty name."

I said, "Then, go to it. You are doing fine."

In these days of pacifism and people who fight capital punishment, laugh at discipline, disregard law and order, and disrespect authority, how we need a generation of people who are loyal and faithful to principle!

Chapter Twenty-Nine

HOLY PLACES AND HOLY DAYS

("Whereupon neither the first testament was dedicated without blood." Hebrews 9:18.

You will notice that Christ has left for us a will. A will cannot be opened unless there is the death of the testator. When Christ died on the cross, His will became valid. Now what He willed to us is ours. You recall that the vail of the temple was rent in twain from top to bottom. This meant that the will was being opened. Before the death of Christ only the High Priest could enter the Holy of Holies. The High Priest represented Jesus Christ. In His will Jesus made it possible for all men to come to God through the vail. Because He has died, His will may be opened. Hence, the Holy of Holies is opened so that all men may come to God. No longer is there a Holy of Holies. Every place is a holy place. Jesus said to the woman at the well, *"God is a Spirit: and they that worship Him must worship Him in spirit and in truth." (John 4:24)* One of the great dangers of our day is having holy places. Bear in mind that the holy places of the Old Testament all pointed to the Lord Jesus Christ. Any time we give attention to a holy place today we take away from the Lord Jesus Christ, for He has come and fulfilled all of the holy days, holy places, etc.

When one day is emphasized above others, the others are de-emphasized. When one task is emphasized above others, the others are de-emphasized. I have often said that the most important sermon is next Sunday's sermon. The most important Sunday is next Sunday. The most important day is today. The most important task is the one that I am doing now. The most important place is the one I am in now. It is very important that we pause to realize that the church building of our day is not the temple of the Old Testament. It is simply as Charles Spurgeon said, "a meeting house," or a meeting place where God's people come and keep comfortable while they do God's work and hear God's Word.

Each of us has heard some well-meaning parent or Sunday School teacher say to some child, "Be quiet! You are in God's house. Be reverent here in God's house." This is unwise teaching. The reason that one should be quiet in church is that it is good manners, not reverence for a building. To teach one to be quiet because one is in church means that he won't have to be quiet when he is in the school assembly meeting. To teach one to be quiet because he is in the house of God de-emphasizes the importance of being quiet in other public gatherings. The reason that a person should behave in church is the same reason that a person should behave in any public meeting. It is just decent and good manners to behave.

So many preachers point to that big sermon out yonder some day – that "convention sermon." So many choir directors rise and shine on that big, special occasion when guests are there from far and near. Then this is true: They de-emphasize the other days, the other choir specials, and the other sermons.

Let every task be a big task. Let every choir special be the most important one ever sung. Let every sermon be the most important sermon ever preached. Make every day be the biggest day ever lived. It is dangerous to look forward to a big occasion and overlook the occasions in between. Let us do our best now, for now is the only real chance we have to serve God. I will do my best where I am now, doing what I am doing now, on the day that I am doing it – today!

Chapter Thirty

HOW HIGH ARE YOUR VALLEYS?

"He is always able to rise to the occasion." How typical this is of our finite minds' estimation of success. *We judge one by the height of his peaks, when the simple truth is that one of the tests of real character is the height of one's depth. It is not how high the mountain top, but how high the valley that counts.* The valley of a mountain range may have higher elevation than the top of a mountain somewhere else; consequently, it matters not how high the peak is, but rather how high the valley is. *Raise your valleys and your peaks will care for themselves.*

It is not how high one can go, but how low he can keep from going. A person is as moral as his most immoral day. He is as efficient as his most inefficient day. He is as deep as his most shallow day. One can be morally clean 364 days a year and yet be an adulterer. One can refrain from robbing banks 364 days a year and yet be a bank robber. One can resist murder 364 days a year and yet be a murderer. It is tremendously important that in one's character he raise the height of his depths, the peak of his valleys, and that he not only "rise to meet the occasion," but refuse to "lower to meet the occasion."

There are many preachers who on a given day, with a big enough crowd, and enough inspiration, can preach great messages. However, the test of a great preacher is not on Easter Sunday, but on Labor Day weekend. The great preacher is the one who gives his best to his people week after week and is the best preacher on his lowest day. The best worker is the one who does his job *every day.* His inspiration comes from within and and is a part of the subconscious.

At this writing Cindy, my youngest child, is eight years of age. She has been afraid of storms all of her life. Oftentimes even a cloudy day will bring tears to her eyes. A few days ago Cindy wrote a little article concerning her fear of storms. She brought it to me. She had written something like this: "I, Cindy Lynn Hyles, do on this 23rd day of June, 1968, quit being afraid of storms. I know that God will take care of me, for He promises to do so. He took care of Daniel in the lion's den; Shadrach, Meshach, and Abednego in the fiery furnace; and He will take care of me. Because of this, I will not be afraid of storms any more. . ."

The article was much longer than that, but all of it was just as well written and serious minded. In less than two hours the worst storm that we had had in weeks was raging. I looked at Cindy, and she was as sober as she could be. I grinned and said, "Are you the little girl that wrote an article a while ago?"

With trembling lips and moist eyes she said, "Yes, sir."

I hugged her and said, "It is a lot easier to promise than it is to fulfill the promise."

It is one thing for a person to vow to do his job well; it is another thing for him to develop the kind of character that subconsciously forces him to do the job well. The doing of right must get on the inside. This means that we will subconsciously do a job well even at our lowest point.

Let us work on the valleys and let the peaks care for themselves. Certainly the peaks are more inspiring. Certainly it is easier to do the job well at the peak, but the ones who will be remembered the longest and will accomplish the most are those who do the unspectacular jobs well when uninspired from without, but subconsciously inspired from within with the kind of character that is more concerned about raising the height of the valleys than raising the height of the mountain.

Chapter Thirty-One

THE SECURITY OF SILENCE

Some of the most beautiful expressions of love are expressed by silence. One may be reading a newspaper while another is putting a crossword puzzle together on the floor, but nothing is being said. Some of the sweetest expressions of love and devotion ever given were given by silence.

Just what does silence say? In the first place, *silence says what the silent man is.* If love exists between two people, silence then is an expression of that love. The bitter heart stores up bitterness in its silence. The selfish heart stores up envy in its silence. The loving heart exudes love in its silence.

Silence between friends says that one's presence is enough. There are millions of places that one could be, but when he chooses from all other places one place, and from all other people one person to share with him that place, even his silence speaks volumes of tender expressions of love. In such silent moments in private sanctuaries one's silence says to his friend, "Your presence is enough." When two people choose to be alone together, each is honored by the other above all men during the moments spent together.

Silence between friends also speaks confidence, for there is no need for one to impress the other. The friendship has already been sealed under God, and there are no more worlds to conquer. This kind of friendship does not take for granted its friend, but rather continues to express love, affection, and gratitude. This expression, however, is not an attempt to impress, for impressions have already been made that will last for life.

This kind of silence says something else. It says, "Dear Friend, I do not have to gain assurance from you of your love. That assurance is spoken to me so often and shown to me so well. My silence with you tells you that I am assured of your love." True friendship need not be reconfirmed daily. It should be perennially expressed and demonstrated. Since *"perfect love casteth out fear,"* often silence can say, "I am assured of your love, and I am assured of your friendship."

True friendship does not decide every day whether it should continue or not. It does not decide every week. It does not decide every month. It does not decide every year. It does not decide even twice! True friendship is God-given and is conditioned by the heart of the lover, not by the traits of the loved. Hence, when God places in the heart of one a true friendship for another, peace, assurance, and security is offered even though not recognized.

Recently I said to one of my daughters, "Daddy loves you, Honey."

She looked up to me and said, "I know it."

Perhaps I had not told her for a few days, but I had so demonstrated that love and expressed that love that even in the silence, I was assuring her that I love her.

Once in a cartoon "Dennis, the Menace" sat down in the barber's chair, looked up at the barber, and said, "What do you say we just don't say nothing today!" As I laughed I thought that perhaps the excessive talking by many barbers is caused by a lack of confidence in their work. This is not to say that a barber should not talk to his customer. It is to say, however, that talk should not have to be forced by the one who applies his trade well.

Though expressions of love, gratitude, and affection are always in order and should be offered, many times the silence of a quiet meal, the silence of the wife sewing while the husband reads the newspaper, the silence that is broken only by the twinkle of an eye, the touch of an arm, or the squeeze of a hand says more than words. Thanks be to God that when people love each other even their silence speaks of that love.

Chapter Thirty-Two

HOW TO BE CLOSE

Tragic but true is the fact that many people live and die and never have close relationships. This is especially true in the life of many pastors. Many grope in darkness hoping to find a close relationship with another and yet never develop the kind of ties for which their dreams have drawn plans.

One of the surest and best ways to develop close ties is to enter into all the relationships of another's life. Though this is perhaps exaggerated a bit, it is none the less true. Many pastors, for example, do not laugh with their people; they only mourn with their people. In so doing they become only a part of the lives of their parishioners. They are only considered or thought about when mourning comes. On the other hand, a comedian only entertains. When one has a party, he invites him. When one wants to laugh, he seeks his company, but in all other areas of life, he is omitted. Hence, one should not confine himself to one area in the life of a friend. Through many years of pastoring, I have tried to laugh with my people, weep with my people, rejoice with my people, and enter into every area of their lives. I want to share with them times of humor, and I want to share with them times of sorrow. When one can entwine himself into every area of another's life, he can become "close" to the other and endear himself as a friend.

The more types of experiences that people can share, the more possibilities there are for times spent in the future. If, as a pastor, I can be a teacher, a comforter, an encouragement, a delight, a strength, etc., then my people can and will associate me with each of these areas of life. The more areas of their lives with which I can become associated, the more needed will I be, the more intimate I can be, and the deeper is the friendship we can develop.

It is vitally important also that we realize that we share these experiences together *while* they are happening. It is important that I, as a pastor, realize that there are people in my congregation with whom I have shared the joys of a wedding, the sorrows of a funeral, the anxieties of an illness, the blessings of a conversion, the thrill of the coming of a new baby, etc. Many share such experiences but miss the blessing and the close ties because they fail to realize the privileges shared while the experiences are taking place.

Chapter Thirty-Three

PERFECT LOVE

"And we have known and believed the love that God hath given to us. God is love; and he that dwelleth in love dwelleth in God, and God in him." (I John 4:16)

While we will not attempt to exegete the above verse, we will think a while about perfect or more mature love. One's love for another may grow until he loves another with all of his heart. What then may he do to offer the object more love? Are we not to continue to have our love for each other increase? Should we "arrive" in our love for our friends? Certainly not! Hence, if you love one with all of your heart, to increase that love you must have a "bigger heart." In other words, our capacity to love must increase.

Not long ago I was out soul winning and came to a certain house where the man of the house was very excited. "Pastor," he exclaimed, "I am glad that you dropped by. I want to show you my new car."

I don't think that I have ever seen a man as excited about a car as was this man. His description of it was such that I thought it must be an air-conditioned Cadillac with television in both front and back seats. "Where is the car?" I asked. "I simply must see it."

The man's face lit up, his countenance brightened, and he clapped his hands with joy because I wanted to see the car. "Come on," he exclaimed. "It is in the back yard. You wait 'til you see it. I have never loved a car like I love this one." Around to the back yard we went and was I ever in for a shock! "Here it is," he exclaimed.

I looked, and to my surprise I saw an old junk heap. The fenders were not the same color as the body; in fact, it looked like a piece of junk.

"What do you think about it?" he asked.

"That IS a car," I replied.

"Isn't that about the prettiest thing you ever saw?" he asked.

I said, "Boy, that is something." (It was "something," and

I was having a hard time figuring out what kind of "something" it was.) I stuttered and stammered trying to keep my conversation in the realm of honesty and truth.

He suddenly saved me from embarrassment by saying. "I made it with my own hands, Preacher. I made it with my own hands."

Then I realized the source of his love. He had gone down to the wrecking yard and picked up a piece here and a piece there, an engine here and a fender there, and actually constructed his own car.

The strange thing about it is that he had a beautiful new car in the garage, but it was one made by Ford or General Motors or Chrysler Corporation. This one, however, was made with his own hands. Hence, he could love it more than the others.

How then may we love someone more? How may our capacity to love someone be increased? We must do things for them. We must invest our lives in them and, like the man with the old car, we will find a love that we have never known before.

Mrs. Hyles and I have four children. We have experienced nearly every Christmas what we had the joy of experiencing again this past year. Our youngest daughter, Cindy, had made a Christmas card for us. This she had made at school. We gathered around the Christmas tree early in the morning to open the gifts. Cindy was most excited, not about the ones she was about to receive, but about the card that she had made for Mommy and Daddy. When I would pick up a gift close to the card, she would jump up and down and clap her hands thinking that perhaps I would find the card too. Though she received a new bicycle for Christmas, she did not exclaim as much over this or her doll or her game or any of her other gifts as she did the card she had made for Mother and Dad. We have all seen a child who deposited a new $15.00 doll in the toy box in preference to a homemade rag doll. Would God that we could find the same truth. Happiness is not in receiving but in giving and the more we actually DO in the making of others and the helping of others, the more our love can increase for them.

Our friends are deserving of more love from us. If they receive it, we have to learn to love more. May our love grow and mature until we can offer to our friends the greatest love ever. Hence, I must do more for others. I must invest more in the lives of others. I must think more of others. I must give more to others. I must sacrifice more for others and in so doing. I will know something of the heart of the fellow who made the car, the child who made the doll, and the girl who made the Christmas card. And I will have attained a point a little closer to what the Master meant when He spoke of "perfect love."

Chapter Thirty-Four

LOVE

I rushed out of my Wednesday evening service and out to the airport in time to catch a 10:00 plane for Atlanta, Georgia, and on to Greenville, South Carolina, where I was to speak for a few days at the Bob Jones University. I got to the airport just in time to get the last seat on the plane. I sat down beside a little lady whose hair was in rollers. She was obviously not dressed for traveling. I could tell, however, that she was of some means, for she had a beautiful diamond ring as well as a diamond pin. Courteously I spoke to her and sat down. The next thing I knew we were landing in Cincinnati, Ohio, for a brief layover. I was awakened by the touch of the wheels on the runway. As I roused, the little lady beside me shocked me by saying, "How could you do what you did?"

Not realizing what I had done, I inquired as to what she meant.

She said, "We have been through a terrible storm. We have been afraid and nervous, and all the time you just snored away. How could you do that during a storm?"

I replied that I did not know the circumstances but perhaps there were at least two reasons why I could sleep through a storm on an airplane: The first reason was that I fly tens of thousands of miles a year on commercial airliners. The second reason I told her was, "My Father owns the airplane."

She looked at me with a puzzled look on her face and said, "Do I understand you correctly? Your father owns this plane?"

"Yes," I said, "He owns the entire Delta Airlines system." This really aroused her curiosity until I continued. "He not only owns the Delta Airlines, but He also owns the American Airlines."

"Do I understand you correctly?" she asked. "You are the heir to the Delta and the American Airlines."

"That is right," I replied. "That is not all. He owns the

Eastern Airlines, the Braniff Airlines, Ozark, United, Continental, and others."

By this time she was completely beside herself in ecstasy. "What an honor," she said, "to ride with such a person whose father is so wealthy." Then she asked the name of my father.

I replied that He was the Heavenly Father. When I said these words, she broke out weeping so that folks all around us could hear her. Her body shook as tears poured from her eyes.

"You must be a minister," she said.

"Yes, I am," I replied, "but I am also a Christian."

Then she told me an unusual story. She had worked her husband's way through college, sacrificing her own college education so that he might attain one. He had become very successful and was the manager of a large firm. With the passing of years, he had become ashamed of his wife because she was less educated than he, and now he was suing her for a divorce. When she heard of this, she attempted suicide. (This was just a few minutes before she got on the plane.) Some friends had brought her to the airport, and put her on the airplane to send her to Atlanta, Georgia, where her sister lived.

She looked at me and continued talking, "Oh sir, how unusual that a minister would sit beside me, Just a few minutes ago I tried to kill myself." Then she looked at me with a look of horror, fright, and anguish and asked, "Sir,. . .does your. . .God. . .love. . .me?"

I will never forget how she looked as she asked me if my God loved her. I was happy to tell her that not only did my God love her, but that I loved her too because Jesus loved her. At twenty-eight thousand feet in the air I told her the wonderful story of Christ and that God did love her. As I went to my hotel room in Atlanta, where I was to sleep for two or three hours before catching a plane to South Carolina, I knelt and prayed, "Dear God, let me love more. The only way people can see Thy love is to see it in me."

In order that our love might be more like His, let us examine a few ways to increase our love.

1. *Remember it is better to love than to be loved.* One can

only guarantee fulfillment by loving, not by being loved. If one's happiness is built upon loving, then it can be controlled, but if his happiness is built upon being loved, it is built upon something over which he has no control. One who loves you can withdraw that love, and there is nothing that you can do about it. *The happiest people and the people whose happiness is most secure are those who find their joy in loving rather than in being loved.*

2. *Love is often unrecognized and unreturned.* As one grows in love he finds himself the possessor of something that the flesh cannot recognize. The carnal mind is at enmity with God, and the flesh cannot determine spiritual traits. Hence, it is entirely possible that the people who love the least will receive credit for loving the most and that the world's greatest lovers will have their love unrecognized by the world. There are many preachers who are described as prophets of love because they never preach against sin, never rebuke their people, etc. On the other hand there are many preachers who are described as prophets of doom and hate who are really full of love for their people. Remember, love is of God, and this old carnal world knows nothing about God and His love. Because of this, the more true love that one has, the less recognition he will get for it. He may find himself being considered unloving by those who have little love but receive praise for being great lovers. Hence, when a person finds his joy and satisfaction in loving, he may have to become accustomed to having that love unrecognized by those about him.

3. *Love gives the object its needs, not its wants.* The love that the world knows is that which fulfills only the wants of its object. The love which God gives is that which oftentimes forfeits its own recognition in an effort to help. Many people who know true love find that oftentimes words of caution and even abruptness must be used to those you love in an effort to help them. The parent who loves his children enough to discipline them may be called an unloving parent. The pastor who loves his people enough to warn them may be called an unloving pastor. Though his love may go unrecognized on earth, it is certainly accepted and recognized

as true love by Him Who is Love.

4. *Love is often heartbroken.* Remember that the higher one goes the lonelier he gets, and the more one loves the more he will feel unloved. He then compares his love for others with that which others have for him, finding that their love for him falls short of his love for them. The consequence is often heartbreak. The compensation for this is great, however, for the more we learn to love on earth, the higher will be our level of spiritual maturity and love in Heaven, and the more love we can offer to the Lord Jesus Christ.

5. *We are not to love because of the object.* "I love her because she is so sweet." "I just love him; he is so nice." These are immature statements that can lead to disappointments.

In the first place, if one's love is determined by the object, it can be also lost when the object changes. If you love her because she is sweet, you will quit loving her when she is sour. If you love him because he is nice, you will quit loving him when he is not nice. However, if you love him because God is love and has given you of His love, his changing will not change your love. Hence, our love should not be because of condition of the loved but because of the condition of the lover.

Another reason why this is important is that if we love because of the object, we will not love those who need loving the most. Jesus loved the unlovable, the unloving, and the unloved. To be like Him, we must do likewise.

6. *Do not let the object stop your love.* If one does not love because of the object, then also he should not stop loving if the object becomes unlovable. I have often said this to the people whom I pastor: "I cannot make you love me, but you cannot keep me from loving you." If one loves because the object is lovable, his love cannot increase unless the object becomes more lovable. In other words, he has no power to increase his love. If, however, one loves because of the love that Christ has placed in his heart, then he can increase his own love by increasing the size of his heart."

7. *Keep all love within its proper bounds.* If disciplined properly, every relationship can be developed to its fullest.

There is love for mother, love for father, love for brother, love for sister, love for husband, love for wife, love for sweetheart, love for friend, etc. Each love should be kept within its own boundaries allowing each relationship to develop to its highest and fullest. It is wise for a person to list his relationships in life. Life is a series of human relationships, and one's happiness is largely determined by the development of each relationship. A list can be made such as the following:

I am a husband to Beverly Hyles.

I am a father to Becky Hyles, David Hyles, Linda Hyles, and Cindy Hyles.

I am a son to Mrs. C. M. Hyles.

I am a brother to Mrs. Earlyne Stephens

I am a pastor to the members of my church.

Now I must develop each of these relationships to its fullest thereby guaranteeing the happiness of each object as well as my own happiness. One does not have to choose between being a good husband and a good father, between a good father and a good friend, or a good son and a good boss. The late Dr. Bob Jones, Sr. used to say, "Duties never conflict." I can be a good whatever I am. God will give me no relationships that I cannot develop to the fullest.

8. *The lover must make all reconciliations.* When there is a strained relationship, it is up to the lover to lead in efforts of reconciliation. Remember the weak is usually too weak to make amends. It is up to the stronger to do so.

9. *By all means, do not work on being loved. Seeking to be loved makes love impossible, for such actions are selfish, and love cannot be selfish.* Selfishness cannot love. Most of the so-called love in our generation is selfish and possessive. It is nothing more than a desire to be with someone who satisfies one of the senses.

Several years ago I noticed in the Fort Worth, Texas, newspaper a picture of a lady bending over the dead form of her husband whom she had just killed. As she picked his head up and put it in her lap she said, "Oh, how I loved you." (I told my wife that I didn't want her to love me that much.)

The average so-called love of today is nothing more than a

desire to be around someone who is pretty or someone whose personality makes us feel good. It is basically wanting to be with someone who likes us. It is selfish and possessive if this is all that is involved. Hence, one should work on his loving and not on being loved. God will take care of giving to us those who love us if we will take care of developing through Him and in Him the right kind of love flowing out of our own hearts.

10. *Express your love.* It is a wonderful thing to be able to express your love. This would simply mean being affectionate. Do you love him? Tell him. Do you love her? Tell her. Has she been a blessing to you? Let her know it. There is far too little tenderness and affection exchanged between friends in our generation. Words of love and affection are always in order if they are set within the proper bounds. Notes and letters to friends we love certainly should be written often. This is a very vital part of friendship and love.

Married people reveal their relationship by the wearing of the wedding band. Athletes wear letter sweaters. Soldiers wear uniforms. Our Lord wanted to give His people something as an insignia of their standing, something by which they could be identified. He did not choose rings for our fingers or a certain piece of clothing to cover our bodies. He simply choose love, for He said, *"By this shall all men know that ye are My disciples, if ye have love one to another." (John 13:35)*

Chapter Thirty-Five

IF I AM YOUR FRIEND

If I am your friend, I would give you all that a friend could give. If I am your friend, I must love you all that I can love. If I am your friend, I must do for you all that I can do. Since it is with my mind that I love you and with my body that I help you, hence, for your sake as well as for mine, I must keep my mind alert and my body healthy. If I abuse my body, I not only do an injustice to myself but also to you, my friend. *Since I am your friend, I pledge you a mind that is healthy and alert so that you can be assured of maximum help. When my mind is gone, I can love you no more. When my body has gone, I can serve you no more. May God help me to keep both well so that I may love you and serve you more and better.*

Chapter Thirty-Six

A YAWN

Not long ago Mrs. Hyles and I were riding with some friends when my wife yawned. After a brief chuckle by all of us I reminded my friends that in many respects a yawn is a symbol of love and affection.

How can a yawn be a symbol of love and affection? There are people before whom we would never yawn. We do not know them that well. We do not feel that much liberty in their presence. On the other hand, there are those with whom we feel at home and who are dear and near enough to us to take us as we are. When around such friends as these, we do not hesitate to express ourselves, even if that expression is a yawn.

Now this little thought is certainly not to advocate rudeness or lack of manners. Certainly there are times when even around my dearest friends, a yawn would be inappropriate, but on the other hand, there are times when with those who are very dear to us we open our mouths and have a big yawn. In so doing we say subconsciously, "I love you and you are dear to me!"

Chapter Thirty-Seven

HOW TO BE A FRIEND

"A man that hath friends must shew himself friendly: and there is a friend that sticketh closer than a brother." (Proverbs 18:24)

Greater love hath no man than this, that a man lay down his life for his friends." (John 15:13)

"Hello, friend" were the words that I spoke recently to a stranger walking down the sidewalk. Immediately I was rebuked. What a careless use of a most sacred word. Add the word "friend" to the words mother, father, son, daughter, and wife. This is the lofty position that it should hold. Too many of us have taken friendship far too lightly.

In the New Testament there are two main words that are translated "friend." One of these words means "comrad, acquaintance, fellow traveler." The other means "one dearly beloved" or "one held precious and dear." Many people never have even one true friend, and few people have many true friends. Cultivating such friendships can become one of life's greatest and most enriching experiences.

1. *Be concerned in being a friend, not in having a friend.* Many would love to have a true friend, but few are interested in being a true friend. Now it would be an unholy motive for one to be a friend in order that he might have a friend. Nevertheless it is true that to have friends one must be a friend. It is far more noble, however, for one to satisfy himself with being a friend. It is better to be a friend than to have a friend. By being a friend one develops character and integrity. One might have a friend without having either character or integrity. Do not spend your life trying to cultivate one's friendship, but rather try to cultivate your own friendship to others. I recently said to someone, "Being loved is life's second greatest blessing; loving is the greatest." Paraphrased it could be said that having a friend is a great blessing, but being a friend is a greater blessing.

2. *Remember what a friend is.* A friend is one who is loved dearly. Do not offer such friendship lightly or casually. It is the kind of friendship which has abiding love and endearment. Just as one should weigh his choice of a mate carefully and wisely, even so should he weigh carefully and wisely the offering of true friendship. This does not mean, of course, that one could not be a friend to many in the usual meaning of friend. It simply means that in the true meaning of friend there should be depth and emotion. One should not assume true friendships unless he can offer both depth and emotion.

3. *Start doing sacrificial things for others.* One of the best places to start in being a friend is living for others. General Booth, the founder of the Salvation Army, sent a telegram to a Salvation Army Convention during his last days because his health would not permit him to attend personally. The telegram simply said, "Others," and was signed, General Booth.

OTHERS

"Lord, help me live from day to day
In such a self-forgetful way,
That even when I kneel to pray
My prayer shall be for others.

"Others, Lord, yes, others,
Let this my motto be,
Help me to live for others,
That I may live like Thee.

"Help me in all the work I do
To ever be sincere and true,
And know that all I'd do for You
Must needs be done for others.

"Let 'Self' be crucified and slain
And buried deep; and all in vain
May efforts be to rise again
Unless to live for others.

"And when my work on earth is done,
And my new work in Heaven's begun,
May I forget the crown I've won,
While thinking still of others."

4. *The need of a friend should be considered your need.*
When a friend is in need, you should be in need. When a
friend has a need, you have a need. This is what the Bible
means by compassion. We suffer *with* those who suffer. We
are admonished to do so in the Scriptures: *"Rejoice with
them that do rejoice, and weep with them that weep."*
(Romans 12:15) As soon as a need is seen in a friend's life, a
true friend will begin attempting ways of filling this need.

5. *Feel as if you are a member of the family.* Often ties of
friendship become closer than some family ties. This is
especially true if the friendship is in the Lord. The Bible
speaks of *"a friend that sticketh closer than a brother."*
(Proverbs 18:24) One should not feel in such a relationship
that he has family privileges, but he should feel that he has
family responsibilities.

It is sad for a person to live and die and never develop such
friendships. One of the great joys of my life is loving people
for whom I would die and having the love of people who
would die for me. This kind of relationship carries with it
responsibilities. These responsibilities are akin to those
caused by family ties. Once some dear friends had a need in
their house. Before I knew it, I found myself purchasing that
need at a considerable expense. As I examine the reasons
behind this purchase, I found the main one was that I
subconsciously felt it was as my need for my house; hence, I
must provide it.

6. *Build up your friend's friends.* Circumstances and
distance often make it impossible for us to be or do for our
friends as we would like. In such cases there is still a way that
we can help provide for the needs of our friends. We may
encourage, train, and help others who are in a position to
provide the needs of our friends. It may mean some unselfish
sacrifice on our part. But if our thoughts are on others, it
matters not where the credit goes; it only matters that the
friend is helped. As a pastor, with many thousands of

members, I find it impossible to do for all of my friends what I would like to do. I can, however, teach their other friends how to be to them what I would like to be and cannot be. This may mean that my friend will feel a closer friendship with the one whom I trained than with me. However, since our goal in this chapter is to be a friend and not have a friend, it still can be reached by using this method.

7. *Enjoy the presence of your friends.* Man is not omnipresent. This means that he can be in only one place at one time, which is quite a handicap to busy people. This means that there are people with whom we would love to spend many hours but with whom we are privileged to spend just a few. When these opportunities come, they should be enjoyed to their fullest.

8. *Spend some time with your friends even in their absence.* One should know who his friends are and those to whom he has given his friendship. It has long been my policy to make a list of people to whom I am a true friend. Many times a month I go over this list and spend some time thinking of and praying for those to whom I am a true friend. This is usually done late in the evening in the hours of meditation. This article is being dictated on a jet plane flying to Tokyo, Japan. I have spent and will spend much time on such a trip thinking of those people who may call me their friend and whom I call my friends. It has long been my policy also to spend some time with and thinking about those who were once my friends and are now in Heaven. I try to remember their lives and thank God for the friendship that I once enjoyed with them.

9. *Do kind deeds for loved ones of departed friends.* It is impossible to do something for those friends who have passed on except as we do it to those of their loved ones who remain. David brought a little crippled fellow by the name of Mephibosheth to his palace to live with him in honor of his departed friend, Jonathan. This was the only way David could do something for Jonathan.

The pastor who preceded me at the First Baptist Church of Hammond, Indiana, is a godly man. When he left Hammond, he assumed a pastorate in California. The miles prevented our church from regularly doing kind deeds for him. Realizing this, we purchased a little house and gave it to his father rent-free as long as he lived. Upon the death of his father, we then offered it to his aunt with the same arrangement. Now to be sure we loved his father and we love his aunt, and we do such gestures because of that love; however, it is also a way of expressing our love for the former pastor in that we express it now to his loved ones.

Friendship is a very serious and sacred thing. It should be treated as such!

Chapter Thirty-Eight

GROWTH IN GRACE

"As newborn babes, desire the sincere milk of the word, that ye may grow thereby." —(I Peter 2:2)

Recently while traveling in a distant state I read of an interview with a coach of a champion football team. He was speaking of the difference between just professional football players and champion football players. He made an interesting comment concerning the difference. He said that all professional football players do 75% of what is expected of them. In other words, to be a professional football player one has to make a fair grade. "Then," he said, "to become a champion one has to master the other 25%." Just making a passing grade is not enough. The difference between just a "pro" and a champion is the mastering of that which is above the calling of duty and above the expected.

The same is true with a Christian. To be just a good Christian is not enough. We should want to become the best Christian possible.

Of course, there are necessary things that one must do in order to grow in grace. He must live in the Word. He must walk with God. He must witness, attend the services of the church faithfully, etc. The following are a few of the rules of growing in grace that have to do with the other 25%.

1. *Do not compare yourself with others.* It is not enough to be a better Christian than someone else. It is only enough to become a better Christian than I now am, and to become the best "me" possible to the glory of God. Suppose one became the best Christian in his class or at work. Having this as a goal he has limited his growth in grace.

Another danger in comparing one's self with other Christians is that normally the one that does the comparing comes out with the "long end of the stick." We are prone to give ourselves the benefit of the doubt, and we might come short of what we could have been simply by wanting to satisfy ourselves as becoming a better Christian than someone else.

2. *It is important to be around those more mature than we are.* Seeing examples is a very important part of growing in grace. Most of us do not have the ability to see intangibles such as ideas, etc. Few people can see or define loyalty, for example. Hence, they must see a loyal person. In order for an average person to comprehend such things as character, integrity, honesty, etc., he must see it incarnate or embodied. This is why it is important for us to be near people whom we would like to emulate.

Here is the mistake of many preachers. We talk about ideas that we can see clearly but which many of our people have a difficult time comprehending. Jesus took great truths and clothed them in simplicity. He spoke of great truths and likened them to getting married, eating bread, drinking water, growing a vineyard, running away from home, losing money, etc.

This is just another way of saying "stay in the right crowd." Yet it does in a sense go a little deeper. It implies staying in a crowd that can challenge your best. It implies association with stronger Christians, at least those stronger in certain points.

3. *Do not have as your main goal to become a better Christian.* This in itself could invite selfishness. Don't forget that *one is to lose himself, not measure himself.* Someone has said that humility is not just thinking little of yourself, but it is not thinking of yourself *at all.* In the realm of Christian love, for example, far too many of us want to love more. Now this is not a bad motive. Much holier than this, however, is the motive to have friends whom we want to be loved more, and if we can somehow increase our l o v e and our capacity to love, our friends can have more love. *Hence it is nobler not to want to be a greater lover, but to want your friends to receive a greater love,* realizing that if our friends do receive a greater love, we must become greater lovers. We then, to an extent, have purified our motive.

4. *Do not measure or display your spiritual growth or size.* Oftentimes in failing to display Christian maturity, one demonstrates it. A Christian, yea, especially a mature Christian, should learn to meet his fellow Christians on their

own level of conversation. Of course, by this I do not mean
base conversation, evil speaking, etc. I simply mean that as
one grows in grace he finds fewer people who know his
vocabulary. The stronger will have to use the vocabulary of
the weaker and much of the time the stronger will have to
live on the level of the weaker. This means that the more a
Christian grows in grace, the lonelier he will become. It also
means that he will hunger for someone with whom to talk
who has obtained the comparable level of spiritual maturity.
This is why oftentimes depth looks shallow and profundity
looks simple. This is why a most mature Christian is often
not recognized as such because he has attained enough
maturity to meet each Christian on his own level.

You recall that Jesus became more lonely as He
approached the top of the mountain. He left the multitude
and went with the twelve. After a while he left nine of the
twelve and took only the three. It was not long until even the
three were asleep, and He was alone with the Father. This
means that the best Christian may be the loneliest Christian
in the world. It also means that he will have to spend much
time with God and that he will have to exert understanding
and strength in his relationship with weaker Christians.

Did you ever stop and think that the burden of
reconciliation always rests with the strong and not the weak?
Realizing that the sinned against will be more spiritual, God
places the burden of reconciliation upon him and not upon
the sinner. Hence, Jesus directs His discussion of being
reconciled to the brother who is stronger, the person sinned
against. When He speaks of being reconciled, He talks to the
one whose brother has aught against him, and not primarily
to the one who has aught against his brother.

If one is so deep that he cannot be understood by the
shallow, how then can he help them? To have these deep
thoughts is fine, and to discuss them with light maturity is
fine, but to speak always on the level of one's own spiritual
attainment is neither profitable nor helpful. In other words,
spiritual growth is of little use unless it can be transferred
into energy and into the service of God and others. To know
a truth simply for the purpose of knowing a truth is vanity.

To seek truth just for self edification is selfishness. To seek
more truth in order to gain strength to help others is
Christlike.

5. *One must remember in Christian growth that the more
he grows in grace the fewer the number that will think him to
be mature.* The more one grows in grace, the lonelier he will
become. Hence, the fewer the people who will understand
him and be qualified to judge his spiritual maturity. Hence,
one of the heartbreaks of Christian growth is that it is often
unrecognized by others. Carnality cannot weigh spirituality.
Hence the mature Christian will have to find his comparison
in being strong enough to help others rather than receiving
their acclaim. The greatest person who ever lived was put to
death on the cross. The more we become like Him the fewer
are those who can understand us. This is why weaker
Christians are often judged to be better Christians. Pride
cannot judge true humility. Carnality cannot judge true
spirituality. The weak cannot properly judge the strong.
Hence, many of the great Christians are seldom recognized as
such.

The flesh, however, does attempt to recognize spiritual
qualities. In so doing, the flesh makes its own humility, its
own love, its own meekness, etc. When the flesh makes its
own qualities, it then tries to satisfy them and meet the
requirements. Most of us are far too concerned with being
considered a lover than about being a lover. Most of us are
more concerned about meeting the fleshly standards of
humility than we are about being humble. Hence, the great
satisfaction of growing in grace will ultimately have to be in
pleasing the Saviour and becoming strong enough to be a help
to others.

Chapter Thirty-Nine

TOO MANY CHIEFS AND NOT ENOUGH INDIANS

"Go to the top" is the cry that every young person hears in our generation. Now the truth is that the "top" is rarely as large as the bottom. The farther toward the top of the pyramid one gets, the fewer stones he will find. The simple truth is that everybody cannot go to the top. Actually, going high is simply relative anyway. If everybody gets high, then high is no longer high. If everyone gets educated, then no one will be educated, for these terms are but relative ones. There was a time when a high school graduate was highly educated and considered more qualified than a college graduate is today. This is not to say that one should not accumulate all of the facts possible. Neither is it to say that one should not receive training. However, it seems to me that *most of our educational institutions are training people to be leaders. Why shouldn't some schools train some students to be followers? When everyone in a society becomes a leader, anarchy is inevitable.* Far too many people who are meant to be Indians are trying to be the chief, and many who are meant to be followers are trying to be leaders. *If we have a need today, it is for good Indians.* Were there no soldiers, there could be no generals. Were there no children, there could be no parents. Were there no employees, there could be no employers. Were there no citizens, there could be no President, and if there are no Indians, there can be no chiefs. Just as God calls some to be leaders, he calls more to be followers. We need the Aarons and the Hurs to hold up the hands of Moses. We need some to go with Saul to Gibeah—a band of men whose hearts God had touched. We need the seven men full of the Holy Ghost to help the apostles in their work. We need the deacons to hold up the hands of the pastors.

God, give us leaders, to be sure, but God, give us followers also. We have said, "Go to the top, go to the top, go to the top," so long that the top is heavier than the foundation, and it is bound to crumble. Let us simply say, "Go as high as you can," but if you can go no higher than the foundation, you may still be used to hold up the entire building. Thank God for the chief, but praise the Lord for faithful Indians!

Chapter Forty

AUTUMN

The time of the year that listens to the echoes of the happiness of summer and girds itself for the coming chill of winter is known as autumn. Perhaps no season of the year does as much to the emotions of men as does autumn. . .Autumn.

Autumn is a season of leaves, when nature dots each leaf with a different color and blends it into a beautiful painting that no artist can capture. It is a season of stacks and piles of leaves and the smell of their burning. . .Autumn.

Autumn is a season of trees, when they, like Joseph of old, put on their coats of many colors and thrill the heart of each observer . . . Autumn.

Autumn is a season of crisp air, when God's air-conditioning is turned on in full blast, causing a spring in the step and a sharpness in the air such as no other season can cause. . .Autumn.

Autumn is a season of melancholy, when mothers who had dreaded summer and the bother of the children find themselves missing Johnny and Susie in the loneliness of a quiet living room after school has snatched them away. . .Autumn.

Autumn is a time of memories—memories of a wonderful summer, the best vacation we ever had, happy meals in roadside restaurants, picnics, ants, flies, car trips, shower baths, and playgrounds. . .Autumn.

Autumn is a time to reflect upon the joys of summer, when the family was closer than at any time of the year. Now we separate to go our several ways with our many activities and varied interests but with memories to keep us together until we pack next year for an ever greater vacation. . .Autumn.

Autumn is a season of explanation, as wide-eyed children tell teachers that this was the best summer ever. They explain with loud voices about the trip to Grandpa's farm, the feeding of the chipmunks in the mountains, and the catching of the biggest fish ever (which must have weighed at least a half pound, and whose picture weighed five pounds, and which weighs twelve pounds in the memory of innocent childhood!). . .Autumn.

Autumn is a season of the sound of footballs and the encouragement of cheerleaders. It is a time when every team is undefeated and has dreams of the championship. . .Autumn.

Autumn is a time of cleaning, when lonely mothers sigh and clean the finger-prints and cluttered closets of little ones whose empty room is suddenly a sanctuary. . .Autumn.

Autumn is a time of tears, when mothers and fathers say good-bye to college students who only last year were in kindergarten. It is a time of wondering where the years have gone, a time of bewilderment as we try to remember just a little of the brief period between kindergarten and college. . .Autumn.

Autumn is a time of the familiar squeak of unoiled school bus brakes, as we see the well-scrubbed children across the street getting aboard. . .Autumn.

Autumn is a time of reunion, when school friends measure each other to see the growth of the summer and when friends forgotten for weeks seem dearer than ever before. Forgotten are the differences of the past year. Forgotten are the arguments on the ball field. Our friendship suddenly is dearer and sweeter than before. . .Autumn.

Autumn is a season when Mom has time to realize what it means to be a mother. She has been so busy being a mother that she has forgotten what being a mother really is. When the chorus of voices has faded toward the school grounds and the shuffling of little feet has left the carpet for the concrete, Mom sits down with emotion and realizes what it is to be a mother. She bows her head in thanksgiving that she has been called to be a woman that "excellest them all." . . .Autumn.

Autumn is a time of weeping. Mother and Dad have wondered for days if little Susie would weep when she went off to school for her first day. Mother has girded little Susie for this occasion and has reminded her to be a good girl and not to cry. Susie, however, forgot to prepare Mother; and as

Susie goes off to school skipping and laughing, it is mother
who sits down and cries, as Dad is bothered with a recurring
sinus condition. . .Autumn.

Autumn is a time when Dad bundles up all the bills to see
how much month is left at the end of the money. He shakes
his head and listens more carefully to the commercials
concerning "Friendly Bob Adams and the Household Finance
Corporation" and ponders his "plight to the poorhouse" as
he prays for God's wisdom and help to provide for his
family. . .Autumn.

But in it all, autumn should be a time of dedication. The
turning of the grass, the dropping of the flower seed, the
dying of the leaves, the fading of the summer all remind us of
the "Corn of Wheat" that fell in the ground two thousand
years ago at Calvary. It reminds us that One had to die that
we might live.

As sure as autumn reminds us of His death, the hope of
spring reminds us of His resurrection; for these same trees
shall bloom again, the same grass shall grow again, these
dying flowers shall blossom again, and our Saviour rose again!

Autumn, finally, is a time to die. It is a time for us, with
the flowers, trees, grass, and nature to die. We should die to
self, die to our own pleasures, and live unto Christ.

We look back in retrospect at the summer and brace
ourselves for the chilling winds of winter. Let us enjoy the
most beautiful season of them all—the season, death—for in
death nature is at its prettiest, Jesus reached His glory, and
we become our best for Him.

Chapter Forty-One

A GOOD NAME

"A good name is rather to be chosen than great riches, and loving favour rather than silver and gold." (Proverbs 22:1)

"A good name is better than precious ointment; and the day of death than the day of one's birth." (Ecclesiastes 7:1)

"Lay not wait, O wicked man, against the dwelling of the righteous; spoil not his resting place." (Proverbs 24:15)

There used to be an old saying, "His word is as good as his signature." The phrase "good name" in Proverbs 22:1 implies more than a name that folks like. It implies a good risk, a good credit name, a good business reputation, integrity, character, honesty, etc. Certainly this is rather to be chosen than great riches. Money cannot give a person a good name, but a good name can get him money. Hence, if one does not have both, it is better to have a good name. It is important to start early in the life of a child teaching him to have such a name.

In the first place, children should be taught to be discreet about indebtedness. Exercise care in going into debt and assuming obligations that cannot easily be met. He should be taught that a debt should be paid on or before the day it is due. He should be taught that anything less than this is dishonesty.

In spite of the fact that care should be exercised in the making of financial obligations, it is, nevertheless, a definite asset for a person to have good credit. I advise young couples to establish good credit immediately upon marriage. Time and again I have encouraged young couples to go to the bank and borrow a hundred dollars, pay it back in a few days; then borrow a hundred and fifty and pay it back in a few days; then borrow two hundred and pay it back in a few days; then borrow two hundred fifty, etc. until they have extended their maximum borrowing power. This is a good idea for a church as well as an individual. One never knows when such a credit standing will come in handy. All of the time he is developing his credit rating.

136

It is also a good idea for a person to buy a few things on credit from companies other than banks. Again, this can be used to help one to establish credit.

If a child is to have a good name, he should be taught to take pride in his family name. Again and again a child should be reminded of his name. A family spirit should be born. This is akin to school spirit. When I was a Paratrooper in World War II I was taught to take pride in the fact that I wore the wings and boots of the United States Paratrooper. I was taught that when I did something wrong I brought reflection against my branch of service. A child should feel the same way about his family name. He should be taught to protect it and guard it with his life.

Another thing that is important concerning the obtaining of a good name is avoiding the appearance of evil. Many names are ruined by people who do no wrong but fail to avoid the appearance of evil. Someone has said, "Your character is what you are; your reputation is what man thinks you are." How sad it is when one's reputation does not measure up to his character. His public relations department has fallen behind the production department. He has the goods but cannot deliver them because of a bad reputation.

A child should also be taught to be dependable and punctual. He should be taught to be on time and meet his obligations and appointments. This is simply another way of saying, "His word should be as good as bond." Promises should not be made lightly, carelessly, or indifferently, but rather, soberly and seriously.

Many people leave their children with nothing but money and not enough character to keep from squandering it. One of the great things that a child can inherit from his mother and father is a good name. If one is so fortunate to inherit this, he should guard it carefully so his children can share it with him.

Chapter Forty-Two

HELPING OTHERS

The only things that you can keep for yourself are those which you give to others.

There is no life so "empty" as the "self-centered" life; there is no life so "centered" as the "self-emptied" life. Miserable is that man who thinks of himself. Happy is that man who thinks of others. Someone has well said, "Happiness is stumbled upon in the pathway of duty."

How may I help others?

1. I must ask myself, "What can I do to help in every need I see?" I must not think, "What can another do to help?" but rather, "What can I do to help?" I must associate myself with the needs of others. Pity is not enough. Sympathy is not enough. Even compassion is not enough. I must always ask, "What can I do to help?"

2. *Another's need must be my challenge.* Two men had passed by the wounded one before the good Samaritan stopped to help. He did not ask, "Should I help?" but rather said, "I must help!" To see another in need was his challenge. This is true not only for the needs of a fellow that is half dead beside the road, but it is true even for the small needs of a friend. I must identify myself with him so that not only will his needs be a challenge to me, but an opportunity. *His* needs must be as *my* needs.

Perhaps being a pastor for so many years makes one feel more identified with others than he would normally feel. I find myself feeling as a part of every family of my church so that when a particular family has a decision to make, I feel that it is "our" decision. When a family has a problem, I feel that it is "our" problem. One will never know the true secret of helping others until he is challenged by their needs.

3. *I must listen for the wants of others.* If that want will not do harm to my friend, I must attempt to satisfy it. Recently I was preaching in a distant state and noticed a beautiful "tie tac" worn by a fellow pastor. I commented to him about the beauty of the "tie tac." The next evening he

handed me a little envelope. As I drove off from the service I opened the envelope and found the "tie tac" that I had admired before. (The next night I bragged on his suit, but to no avail.)

4. *I must determine the answer to another's needs even if I am not asked.* Of course, I will not offer the answer unless I am asked to do so. I must not appear to be a know-it-all, yet I must always attempt to find the answers to the needs of others.

A few years ago I was leaving for a trip to the Middle East when a friend of mine said with a smile on his face, "Jack, I would suggest that you not go to Milan, Italy."

I inquired as to the reason for this suggestion, and then he said, "That is the location of the 'Leaning Tower' and knowing you as I do, you would try to straighten it up while there."

This is my point: I must remind myself, however, to be very careful not to volunteer my solutions, but at the same time, I must always have tried to think of a solution in order to be able to help when asked.

5. *I must not consider what others have done for me.* I am debtor to all men. Whether or not someone would do it for me has nothing to do with my decision to help him. The Apostle Paul said that he was debtor to all men, to the Jew, to the Greek, to the Barbarian, yea, to every man. I, too, am such a man. I am a debtor to those who love me just because they love me. I am a debtor to those who hate me because they need me. Our Lord reminds us that it is no longer an eye for an eye or a tooth for a tooth, but we are to bless those who curse us, pray for those who despitefully use us, and love those who hate us. This is the law of Grace and the law of Love. I must not help others because they help me; I must help others because they need help. My motivation should not be caused by external stimuli but internal love and compassion. *The unkind may need me more than the kind, the ugly more than the pretty, the bad more than the good, the weak more than the strong, so I must remember never to let what others do for me motivate my deeds for them.*

6. *I must be careful that what I do is best for others and*

not what others think I should do for them. My satisfaction should not come from satisfying others but from helping others. My goal should not be to be loved and admired by others but to help others. Hence, I must not always do for another what he thinks should be done for him. This means that oftentimes those whom I love most will understand me the least. It means sometimes the ones for whom I do the most will think I do them harm. It may not be until we are in Heaven that my brother will understand that I have helped him, but help him I must, and help him I will! My goal is not to please him but to help him. To be sure, to please him is a welcome bonus; to help him is the great reward.

7. *I must wait for vindication when misunderstood.* The One Who helped others the most was crucified, misunderstood, hated, and rejected of men. Could it be that the more I become like Him the more I, too, will be misunderstood, rejected, and hated of men? When, and if, I am so honored to be counted worthy to suffer with Him, may it be because I, with Him, have tried to help others. And may I leave to Him the vindication and the retaliation.

I know a preacher who was hated by another. He sought no retaliation, but instead did anonymous favors for his enemy. In due time he was completely vindicated, and his enemy fell into sin and reproach. *"Vengeance is Mine; I will repay, saith the Lord." (Romans 12:19)*

I must help those who need help the most. The one who does me evil is in the most need of my help.

8. *I must not be happy about my vindication.* It has been a wonderful thing through the years to watch the hand of God upon my ministry. Miraculous things have happend as God has vindicated His Word and soul winning through the years. Unfortunate things have happened to people who have lifted up their hands against God's anointed. Though I rejoice in God's protecting hand, I must not rejoice when misfortune falls to others as God vindicates me. I must remember to let God care for the vengeance, and I must comfort my enemies even while they suffer such vengeance. I must be happy about God's protection of me, but I must not be happy when another suffers.

9. *I must claim wisdom to help others.* I do not always know the needs of another. Since his wants may not be his needs, and since I, too, am limited by human frailties, I must seek divine help and wisdom to determine his needs. I have this promise from the Holy Spirit: *"If any of you lack wisdom, let him ask of God, That giveth to all men liberally, and upbraideth not; and it shall be given him." (James 1:5)* I must claim this promise. Without it, I could misinterpret the needs of others and do them harm instead of good.

How then may I get wisdom? I may get it by reading diligently the book of Proverbs, which is the book of wisdom. I may get it by fellowship with those who are wise. In fact, there is a bit of wisdom that I can get from every man. Every man knows something that I do not know; I must probe until I find it; hence, all men are my teachers.

OTHERS

"Lord, help me live from day to day
In such a self-forgetful way,
That even when I kneel to pray
My prayer shall be for others.

Others, Lord, yes, others,
Let this my motto be
Help me to live for others,
That I may live like Thee.

"Help me in all the work I do
To ever be sincere and true,
And know that all I'd do for You
Must needs be done for others.

"Let 'self' be crucified and slain
And buried deep: and all in vain
May efforts be to rise again,
Unless to live for others."

Chapter Forty-Three

GENTLENESS

In Galatians 5:22 we find mentioned the fruit of the Spirit. Notice very carefully that this does not say the "fruits" of the Spirit. Each of these graces or qualities is a portion of one "fruit." Oftentimes people erroneously teach that soul winning is only one of the fruits and try to prove their point with Galatians 5:22. You will notice, however, that soul winning is not a part of the fruit of the Spirit. Neither is it a part of the gifts of the Spirit. Every Christian is to be a soul winner.

Let's use the simple illustration of a fire department. Every fireman is to put out fires, but there is a certain way that firemen should behave. They should have clean uniforms and clean fire trucks. They should know the streets of the city. They should be courteous. They should be physically strong, etc. No one, however, would say that a fireman should spend all of his time doing calisthenics just to be physically strong. Neither would one say that having a clean uniform would substitute for putting out fires. It is understood that every fireman is to put out fires, but there are some things that firemen should do as they put out fires and as firemen.

The Great Commission, *"Go ye into all the world, and preach the gospel to every creature,"* is given to every Christian. Soul winning is not one of the gifts; it is every Christian's job. However, as we win folks to Christ, there is a fruit that we are to have, and that fruit is the fruit of the Spirit as mentioned in Galatians 5. As we go soul winning we are to have love. As we go soul winning we are to have meekness. As we go soul winning we are to have joy, etc.

One part of this fruit is gentleness. Gentleness is not a substitute for soul winning, but is a supplement for soul winning. In other words, we are to be gentle as we serve God.

If a person refuses to obey Christ in carrying out the Great Commission, he will have to find a synthetic fruit. One who works mainly at having love will have a synthetic kind of love. One who works mainly at having any part of the fruit of

142

the Spirit will find it something that is tacked on and not built-in. When one gets the fulness of the Holy Spirit for soul winning, he will then have an inbred fruit of the Spirit. This kind will not fail him in a crisis. It is a part of him. Such is the case about gentleness.

1. There are several words in the Greek which are translated "gentleness." One is a word which comes from two words which mean "into" and "fitting." Putting them together we come up with "fitting into" or better still, "appropriate." We must learn to be appropriate. This would include manners, ethics, etc. Christian people should know how to dress to fit the occasion. They should know the proper eating manners and social graces. They should learn to be appropriate.

Much care should be taken that in teaching such things we do not rear children to become "snobs." The having of manners should not be an end in itself but rather a means to an end. We must remember that manners are only customs. The Japanese sits on the floor while he eats. When eating in a Japanese home one should do likewise. To set a strict, rigid rule for manners is unwise. All such things are relative and one should be more interested in being appropriate than in adhering to a rigid set of rules that make him offensive. However, one should know what is considered proper and be able and willing to be appropriate as long as being appropriate does not mean the giving up of conviction.

I was in a certain home recently as a guest at a meal. It was a poor home and one inhabited by godly people, yet people who did not know what normally would be considered good manners. The head of the house grabbed the fork in one hand, the knife in the other, put his elbows on the table, lowered his mouth three or four inches from the plate and began to "shovel it in." Now I was not equipped with the talent necessary to copy him. I did, however, ask if he would give me permission to divide my biscuit and sop the gravy. (Now in most circles this would not be proper.) Not only did he give me permission, but he said, "You are a regular fellow. I like you! You are not like most preachers!"

The story is told that Abraham Lincoln was once eating at

a formal banquet when a fellow next to him poured his coffee into his saucer and drank from the saucer. The elite audience was shocked at such a gesture. Abraham Lincoln realized the man's embarrassment and likewise poured his coffee into his saucer and began to drink from it. Perhaps the greatness of Abraham Lincoln is manifested in such acts as this as well as in his statesmanship and leadership.

I have often thought that perhaps real education is knowing enough to fit into any situation that is moral and not feel uncomfortable or cause others to feel uncomfortable. If one's education allows him only to behave with the educated, he is yet lacking. On the other hand, for one to be unwilling because of prejudice to know how to fit in gracefully with the educated also shows a sign of character deficiency. We must remember, however, that the purpose of all of this is not that we be good appropriate people. This in itself would be an unholy motive. We must remember the purpose is that all classes of people need help, and by learning the true meaning of the word "gentleness" we may not only be able to reach all but also to help all.

The rich man needs help as well as the poor. The elite one needs help as much as the uncouth. The up-and-outers need help as well as the down-and-outers.

I tell my boy that I want him to be at home on the ball field, when company comes, at church, at a symphony concert, or at the fishing hole. Appropriate manners, appropriate dress, appropriate conversation, etc. should be a vital part of every child's education. One would not want to wear a tuxedo on a fishing trip. Neither would he want to wear a leather jacket to a wedding.

This is the first use of gentleness in the Bible. This particular word is found in Titus 3:2, *To speak evil of no man, to be no brawlers, but gentle, shewing all meekness unto all men."*

2. There is another word translated "gentleness" in the Bible. This could be called "firm care." This is found in II Timothy 2:24, *"And the servant of the Lord must not strive; but be gentle unto all men, apt to teach, patient."* Gentleness is not weakness. It is not even what the average person calls

meekness. It is not softness. Gentleness is firmness. Gentleness is strength. It is love wrapped in character. It is as the nurse with the child. She does not yield to the child's whims but loves the child enough to be firm to do things for the healing of the child. Gentleness is the teacher handling the slow student. It is not the overlooking of the student's weaknesses, but the firm leadership of the student that he may do better. Gentleness is the parent handling the trying child. It is disciplining with a tear for the good of the child. This is the reason that a child needs a mother and dad. The softness of a mother with the firmness of a father are chosen by God to be used as a beautiful blend in the rearing of children.

3. Still another word used in the New Testament for gentleness could be translated "evenness." We have learned as we have discussed the subject of meekness that meekness is not looking down upon or up to anyone, not thinking ourselves better or worse than anyone, not thinking of ourselves at all, but looking at everyone equally. *Now gentleness could be called "the acting out of meekness." Meekness is the feeling that we have to all men; gentleness is the acting out of that feeling.* It is the laboratory of the theory of meekness. In other words, there should be an evenness about our handling of people. We should be as nice to the poor as to the rich. We should be as courteous to those who need our help as to those who help us.

How can we do this and live Bible gentleness? First, we can learn to know all types of people. This would necessitate our being with all types of people. For a person to become a well-rounded, gentle Christian, he must learn to walk with the illiterate and also with the scholar without feeling uneasy or causing uneasiness. To do this one must plan to rub shoulders with all classes in order that he may know their needs, their heartbreaks, their sorrows, their joys, their victories, and their defeats. For one to limit his contacts to any certain class of people is to limit his opportunity to help people.

Then one must learn to do many things. The pianist could well afford to learn to play sports. The sportsman could wisely learn something about music. One's interest must be varied if he is to help people in all walks of life.

We should also read a variety of things. For many years now I have read such magazines as the *Nation's Business, National Geographic, Reader's Digest,* and even *Better Homes and Gardens.* (Yes, you read it right.) I have read sports magazines and other educational publications. All of this is simply to reach people and help people in all walks of life. Since I have tried to help so many ladies, I should know something of their interests. Since I want to help businessmen, I must know something of the business and economic condition of our nation.

There are many other things that would lead a person to be able to help people in all walks of life and all classes. It is important, for example, that every child be influenced by a mother and father. It is important that we learn to keep our hobbies as hobbies and not get the cart before the horse. And of course, it is most important that we walk daily with Him. He could talk to a ruler one day and a fallen woman at the well another. He could speak intelligently about bread to the baker, about the stars to the astrologer, about water to the woman, about a vine to the husbandman, about truth to the philosopher, about sheep to the shepherd, about plowing to the farmer, about mediation to the lawyer, about fishing to the fisherman, and about marriage to the lover. He is our example of gentleness.

Chapter Forty-Four

THE CHRISTIAN'S CABINET

The wise man said, "...*in the multitude of counsellors there is safety.*" Even the President of the United States realizes this and chooses for himself a group of men whom he calls his cabinet. These men are experts in different fields in which the President has to make decisions. He meets with them for counsel and advice.

Dr. Bob Jones, Sr. said, "You can borrow brains, but you cannot borrow character." Perhaps it could be said that one who does not need to borrow character will inevitably borrow brains.

Each person should have several people on his cabinet. "*For by wise counsel thou shalt make thy war: and in multitude of counsellors there is safety.*" *(Proverbs 24:6)* "*Without counsel purposes are disappointed: but in the multitude of counsellors they are established.*" *(Proverbs 15:22)* "*Where no counsel is, the people fall: but in the multitude of counsellors there is safety.*" *(Proverbs 11:14)*

Pity the know-it-all. Pity the person who has come to the place where he thinks he does not need advice and counsel. Of course, one should be very careful that he chooses only Christian counselors. "*Blessed is the man that walketh not in the counsel of the ungodly...*" *(Psalm 1:1)* It is dangerous and unwise for a high school student to seek the counsel of so-called senior counselors if they are not Christians. To be sure, the students should not be rude to them, and they should listen to them but not consider the things that they have to say.

Now who should be on one's cabinet?

1. *The Pastor.* Before making any serious decision certainly one would want to counsel with his pastor. This could be done oftentimes in a private conference. Other times simply a telephone conversation will do, but the wise person will seek the counsel of his pastor before making life's great decisions. This is the reason that parents should build the pastor up in the minds of their children. The day may

come when a young person will have to have the help of a
counselor. It well might be that the pastor is the only one
that can help. At that time the parent will be glad that he has
taught his children to respect the pastor. The parents who
criticize the pastor at home are teaching them not to go to
the pastor when they need his counsel and advice, and in the
long run, they do irreparable harm to the child. When the
child needs the counsel of his pastor, he will not seek his
advice nor follow it. Many lives could have been saved had
parents been more careful in their conversation about the
pastor around their family circle.

The godly pastor longs to help his people. He will be glad
to counsel with you. Seek his advice. He should be on your
cabinet.

2. *Choose someone with the gift of wisdom.* The Apostle
Paul speaks in his first letter to the Corinthian church about
the gifts of the Spirit. One of these gifts is the gift of wisdom.
God graciously gives to some a double portion of
discernment and wisdom. Each person should seek out such
people and have one or more on his cabinet. One should not
be afraid to seek their advice. Such a person is inevitably
interested in the lives of others as this trait is inseparable with
this gift.

3. *A sincere friend.* "Ointment and perfume rejoice the
heart; so doth the sweetness of a man's friend by hearty
counsel." (Proverbs 27:9) This should not be someone given
to extravagant flattery, but who is friend enough to be
honest, sincere, and frank. This counselor should be one who
knows you well, loves you dearly in spite of your faults, and
would counsel you for your own good and not for his own
personal benefit of standing with you.

4. *Someone who is successful in your field or in the field
you plan to enter.* If, for example, a young person is going to
be a school teacher, he should also have a cabinet member
who is successful in the teaching profession. To be sure this
person should be a Christian. Every person should have such
a cabinet member.

5. *Parents (if Christians).* Each child should feel that he is
able to go talk to his mother and father. Oftentimes parents

say such things as, "You don't know how hard it is for kids to talk to their parents," or "The hardest person to talk to is someone in your own family." This should not be so, and it need not be so. There are several things parents can do to avoid such a catastrophe, and it is definitely a catastrophe!

(1) *Start early in the child's life having regular talks with the child.* This will help develop an at-homeness between the parent and the child. One of the problems concerning the line of communication between parents and child is the fact that we wait so long to start developing such habits that we find it awkward to do so. Because of this, regular talks should begin early in the life of the child.

(2) *Nothing should appear to be funny to the parent.* Appear to be interested. Their problems may seem trivial to you, but they are dead serious to your children. If they feel that you think the problems are humorous, they will not return to you with their problems the next time. Be interested, listen carefully, and never make light of their conversation no matter how trivial it may seem.

(3) *Treat them as adults.* Never talk about their love as being puppy love, and never let the child feel that you look down at him as he shares with you his problems.

(4) *Listen carefully to everything they say.* Let them present their case. Do not interrupt with premature advice. Be sure the entire case has been presented before the jury gives its verdict. Many times this is the main thing that a child wants—just someone to listen to him.

(5) *Always have time for private conversation with the child.* If the parent does not take time for the child when the child is young, the child will not take time for the parent when he is old. Do not make the child feel that you are rushed. Give him ample time and let him know that he is tremendously important to you.

(6) *Be on the lookout for times when the child might want to talk to his parent.* Sometimes the young

person might be a bit timid to talk to Mom and Dad. Oftentimes a wise mother or father will suggest that they talk as he sees the need arising in the life of a child. Be on the lookout for such times and give ample opportunity for them to discuss their problems with you.

(7) *Always be confidential.* When the child talks to the parent in confidence, it should be kept in strict confidence. Once the parent has betrayed this the child will be reluctant to share his problems with the parent again or to return to the parent for counsel.

(8) *Build up the child's confidence in the parent.* There should be a definite understanding that Mom and Dad are big and important people. A child should be trained to believe that Dad's advice is as good as the school teacher's and that Mom's is as good as any special counselor's. Do not make such statements as, "Dad is not an expert here," or "You had better go to someone smarter than me." Lead the child to believe that Mother and Dad are loving experts who can give advice worthy of being followed.

We have been discussing the Christian's cabinet. On that cabinet should be the Pastor, the parents, someone with the gift of wisdom, sincere friends, and people successful in your chosen field. Take a moment now and list your cabinet. Write their names on a piece of paper. Keep the list accessible. When there is a decision to make, go to your cabinet members and ask their counsel and advice. Of course, the decision is yours, but it should not be made without consulting the cabinet.

Chapter Forty-Five

EDUCATION

"Wisdom is the principal thing: therefore get wisdom: and with all thy getting get understanding." (Proverbs 4:7)

"To give subtilty to the simple, to the young man knowledge and discretion." (Proverbs 1:4)

"My son, attend unto my wisdom, and bow thine ear to my understanding." (Proverbs 5:1)

"How much better is it to get wisdom than gold! and to get understanding rather to be chosen than silver!" (Proverbs 16:16)

"He that getteth wisdom loveth his own soul: he that keepeth understanding shall find good." (Proverbs 19:8)

Education is the acquiring of knowledge and the wisdom with which to use it properly. Few things have been as perverted in our generation as the concept of what education really is.

1. *Formal education is just one form of education.* To be sure, it is a very vital one, but it is not the only one. There are those among us, sad to say, who feel that the only way to acquire an education is through formal training. Some have even made a god of formal education and have fallen into the pit of j u d g i n g every person by how many schools and what schools he has attended. Someone has said, "There is no fool like an educated fool." Perhaps an educated fool is one of those persons who feels that one's social standing should be determined by the number of hours he has spent in formal training. The truth is that some of the most educated people that I have ever met had very little formal training. This is not to discount the importance of formal training; it is simply to attempt to keep others from discounting the importance of the acquiring of knowledge and wisdom from every source and not just one. How tragic it is to find someone so self-centered and so perverted that he feels the only way to acquire knowledge is in the use of the particular methods he used. Someone has said, "The only difference

between college graduates and those who have never been to college is that they are uneducated in different subjects."

2. *Education is more than knowledge.* How tragic it is when one comes to a time in life when he feels that becoming an educated person is simply to become a dictionary with a fleshly binding. A truly educated person has more than an accumulation of facts. He has the wisdom with which to use those facts. When this wisdom is obtained one also becomes tolerant to those with fewer facts. Someone has said, "The most dangerous thing in the world is a man with a brain that is well educated but who does not have enough character to know how to use it.

3. *All people are educated to a degree.* Of course, some are educated more than others, and the truth is that some of the most educated people whom I have ever known were very limited in formal training. For example, some of the most successful preachers in history have been men with little formal training. In some cases, the pastors of the world's largest churches are men whom some would consider unqualified to pastor and whom smaller churches would not even consider. This is not to minimize the importance of formal training, for certainly, the usual case should allow for such training. We are simply pleading for the case of allowing some possibility that a person without the formal training could be very educated. The average pulpit committee would not consider a man with the formal training of a Dwight Moody or Billy Sunday. How sad!

4. *Successful people without the formal training are the exception rather than the rule.* It is usually best for young people to pursue the normal preparation required for a certain field. I recommend to my young men who are called to preach that they go to college, and if possible, seminary.

A young man once went to a seminary professor on his first day in school and said, "I want to preach."

The seminary president asked, "Do you have any sermons?"

"No," replied the young preacher, "but God will put the words in my heart."

The president then very wisely said, "All right, go down to a certain street and a certain place and I will have an appointment for you to preach there on the street corner Saturday afternoon."

The young man looked at the seminary president with a puzzled expression and said, "Why sir, that is in the Mexican area of town. Those people speak Spanish."

"Well," replied the president, "Since God is going to put the words in your heart, He may as well put Spanish as English."

Someone once said to a famous preacher, "God doesn't need your education."

The preacher wisely replied, "God doesn't need your ignorance either."

Hence, it is the usual and safest course for young people to pursue the formal education generally required for success in their chosen fields. There must be, however, room allowed for the success of those who have climbed the ladder without this particular form of training.

5. *Taste is not a sign of education.* One of the most disgusting things in the world to sane people is to find someone who thinks he is more educated than another because he likes a certain kind of music, a certain kind of art, etc. These things are relative. There is no such thing as better music or better art. It so happens that I like what is commonly called better music and better art, but who is to say which is better of the things that are purely relative. In our day a fellow can throw a tomato on a canvas, squirt some mustard all over it, pour on a little black pepper, stir it beyond recognition and call it modern art. One can get an old rim of a tire, beat it with a hammer, cover it with canvas and unveil it as sculpture. Many people develop superiority complexes and even an excess of pride because they have the idea that education is in developing the certain tastes and appreciations that they have been brainwashed to believe are the criterion of being an educated person. Folly!

The question then comes, "How can we become educated persons?" One way is to know the Bible. The Bible is the basis of truth. Nothing is true which is contrary to the Word of God. Not only will the knowing of the Bible make a person more educated, but the reading of the Bible will improve his English, literature appreciation, and refinement.

Another way to become an educated person is to watch and observe great people. Some great people are teaching in schools. Many are not. Regardless of where greatness is found, one should avail himself of the opportunity of observing it.

Someone told me this when I was a kid preacher. I subsequently invited every great man I could to preach in my churches. What a tremendous contribution this has made to my life. What a privilege it has been for me to observe greatness and watch great people. I trust that some of it has "rubbed off."

Another way to obtain an education is by reading. Many have said that formal education is simply teaching a person how to read. To say the least, one's education can be extended by constant use of books and good literature. It is wise for one not only to become well educated in his field, but somewhat educated in almost every field. For the person who has little or no opportunity for formal training, reading affords him all of the the opportunities necessary for success.

Then there is the necessary thing of studying hard in school. The wise youth will make the most of his days in school. He will study hard and prepare himself for life. One of the main reasons for this is that life's habits are formed so early. One's character is molded at such at early age. One who works hard in school will probably work hard after graduation. One who just barely gets by in school will barely get by after he graduates. During school days habits are made and character is molded that will determine the success or failure of a life. Hence, every person in school should do his best and accumulate every possible bit of knowledge so that he might be used to his fullest in life.

One of the finest ways to become educated is through travel. As often as possible a person should avail himself of travel opportunities. When such opportunities arise, care should be taken in the planning of activities so as to make the trip educational as well as a pleasure.

One of the most important things in the securing of an education is the wise choice of the proper college. A college should be chosen that builds character as well as minds. It should be remembered that the type of training to be received is far more important than the prestige that comes with the diploma. Nothing is as highly exaggerated as the accreditation, etc. It is too bad that many parents are more concerned about their children getting talent than character. When a person develops character, he will develop the talent necessary to succeed in his chosen field. Oftentimes a talented person thinks he can make it without hard work, and consequently, runs from character. Character without talent will acquire the talent necessaary. Talent without character is usually lazy and flabby. A college should be chosen on the basis of what it will do for the young person, not what opportunities it will give him after he graduates. The right kind of character will make the opportunities and seize upon them. Education is not the acquiring of a chance, or the acquiring of an opportunity; it is the acquiring of character and knowledge. These should be the things considered in choosing a college.

In these days when communism and almost every kind of "ism" in the world can be found on college campuses, it is also vitally important that great consideration be given to Christian colleges and universities, and much counsel and advice should be received from successful spiritual people concerning the choice of a college. Thousands and thousands of godly parents have worked, saved, and even sacrificed in order that their child might get what "they were not privileged to get"—an education. Through blood, sweat, and tears they provided an education for their child, only to have his faith shaken in the Word of God and the principles he had learned at the feet of his mother and father. This is nothing more than robbery and deceit on the part of colleges and universities. Especially is this true when an institution carries the name of Christian and yet breaks down the Christian faith. In the opinion of this author it is better for a young person to go to an out-and-out secular college, where he will have his guard up and not be deceived, than to be led to believe that the school is Christian, but where he walks away with a diploma that he did not have and without faith in the Word of God which he did have.

It is a good idea for parents to find the names of colleges that not only are places of culture, refinement, and education but places where the Word of God is honored, believed and taught. Parents should start early in the life of a child by helping create in his mind a desire to go to that college or university.

Some of the most highly educated people that I have ever known have many degrees. On the other hand, some of the most highly educated people that I have ever known have no degrees. May God give us His leadership and wisdom with which to utilize every opportunity of life in receiving an education. Then may He give us enough sense to realize that one may achieve success and become educated without following the particular route that we followed.

Chapter Forty-Six

REARING CHILDREN

As a boy I often spent time throwing a ball up and catching it in the front yard. When my dad would walk out of the house, I would ask him to play catch with me, but he was always too busy. I can recall as a little boy saying to myself, "I will be glad when I grow up to be a daddy. I will take time to play catch with my boy."

Now for nearly seventeen years I have been a daddy. I trust I have been the kind pleasing to God and helpful to my children.

When my first daughter, Becky, was born, I stood at the window of the maternity ward with a big, loose-leaf Scofield Reference Bible in my hand. I showed it to Becky through the window, and explained to her that this was the Bible and that the Bible was the Word of God. I did this to the delight and amusement of onlookers. The first night that Becky was home from the hospital I talked to her about the plan of salvation. I took her from the Garden of Eden to the New Jerusalem, and though she seemed unimpressed, I continued doing so until she was old enough to be saved.

Oh, for America to return to the kind of homes that rear children with character and integrity!

1. *The rules should be clearly defined at an early age.* When our children were yet infants, learning how to walk, we took them on a guided tour of the house. We pointed to the things they were not to touch and said, "No, no, no, no, no." We taught them to say, "No, no, no, no, no." Then when one of the off-limits things was touched, the child was spanked. I am talking about a one-year old. Hence, we never had to move any vases off our tables. Our children didn't rearrange our furniture or our schedule. They were taught very clearly what the rules were, and they have abided by those rules through the years.

2. *Expect rigid adherence to the rules.* For example, at our house eleven o'clock is curfew time. Unless special permission is granted, this is always the time for the youngsters to be at home. One minute after eleven o'clock is too late and causes disciplinary measures to be taken.

3. *Strict punishment should be given when the rules are broken.* The punishment should be worse than the reward is good. A child should always be taught that doing wrong is a bad bargain. If a youngster can stay out an hour late and get nothing but a spank on the wrist, he will decide that another hour with his girl friend is worth a spank on the wrist. However, if being an hour late keeps him from going out with his girl friend for a week, he will be on time from then on.

One Saturday afternoon before Christmas, my boy David went Christmas shopping. He was to be home by three o'clock. He came in eleven minutes late. I took him to his room and then explained why I was going to spank him. I bent him over my knee and gave him a good thrashing. I sat him beside me and asked him, "Now, little man, just what were you doing that was so important that you could not be on time?"

With quivering lips and tear-dripping eyes, he murmured, "I was getting your Christmas present gift wrapped."

To be sure, I felt like a heel, and yet, I would spank him again. A rule is a rule and it should be kept. In the long run we will make better children and law-abiding adults if we will impress upon them the importance of obeying the rules.

4. *Just what is a spanking?* I have never felt that a child should be spanked immediately or in public. It should not be the parent giving vent to his anger or release to his emotions. It should be a time of reminding the child that wrong does not turn out right and that he must pay for the doing of it.

With our children I have followed this procedure: When the child does something deserving a spanking, I say sternly but quietly, "Go to your room." I then follow him to his room, sit down across from him, look him straight in the eye, and explain to him what he has done that is wrong. I then ask him to explain to me the wrong that has been committed. When he knows what he did and I am convinced that he knows, I then say to him, "Bend over Daddy's knee." This he does under his own power. In the case of the girls, they are asked to pull up their skirts. I then proceed to spank and spank hard. How long do I spank? I spank until the will of the child is broken. When the child is crying and is obviously broken hearted, I cease the spanking.

When the spanking is finished, I ask the child to sit across from me again and explain to me again why I spanked him. After a brief word of prayer asking God's forgiveness, I then leave him in the room by himself to think about what he has done. This period of meditation usually lasts ten or fifteen minutes. Hence, from the time that the act is committed until the time the procedure is over is about thirty minutes. This makes a spanking an ordeal. A few spankings of this kind will take the place of many of the little temper tantrums that parents usually have and refer to as spankings.

By the time our children got eight or ten years old, spankings were very infrequent. They knew what they were. They knew what to expect, and they knew they would get what they expected if they did wrong. Wrong had become very distasteful by this time.

People often ask with lamentation what is wrong with our generation. "Why the anarchy?" It does not take the thoughtful person long to decide where the trouble lies. It was only about twenty years ago that a new theory came out that we should not spank children. Now we have raised that generation. They have become anarchists, hippies, hoods, and lawbreakers. They have been taught as infants that wrong is not punished. They have been reared by this philosophy. Now we realize what we find in God's Word will work.

5. *Keep the communication line open between parent and child.* It should always be understood that the child can talk to the parent. Questions about life should be directed to the parent. The child should feel that Mom and Dad are always interested in his problems and always willing to talk about them.

The following is a letter received in 1968 from my thirteen-year-old son, David, showing the importance of the father-son relationship!

Dear Dad,

I am the luckiest boy in the world to have parents like you and Mom. I think you are the *greatest* man in the world, and I wouldn't trade you for any other father in the world.

In my eyes, Dad, you are the greatest preacher in the world. A lot of times at school I hear kids talking about their old man. I couldn't picture a kid of yours doing that because you take us places, buy our clothes and food and other things, and take care of us.

In my opinion you are the greatest Christian and soul winner and preacher in the world. And I'm always proud to tell my teachers and friends at school about you. You spend time with me. Not many fathers do that and I appreciate it.

I want to thank you for the things you got me in Japan and for taking me to Washington. I really enjoyed it. I also want to thank you for all you do for me.

If I can be half as great a man as you, I'll be glad. I love you and thank God for having a dad like you. And I'm proud you're my dad and love you as much as I possibly could.

I love you.

Your son,
Dave

P.S. I pray that you will always preach like you do and be as good a Christian as you are.

Enjoy this statement because I'll probably never say it again. I'm proud to have a good-looking dad.

Now you will read a copy of the answer from Dad to son:

Mr. David Hyles
8232 Greenwood
Munster, Indiana

Dear David:

I have read and re-read your recent letter to me. There are several things that came to my mind as I read it.

1. I am honored to have a son who shows gratitude. One of the most important things in life is to be grateful. As a preacher's son, and later as a preacher, many things will be given to you, and much attention will be showered upon you. It will be easy to take things for granted and to think the world owes you something. All the world owes any of us is a chance to

succeed, and this you will have. I am glad that you take time to write thank-you notes and that you are grateful.

2. Naturally I am glad that you have confidence in me. I have prayed for you from the day that I heard that you were coming to our home. I have prayed for God to make me the right kind of example. I pray He will help me to continue to be the kind of example of which you can be proud.

3. You do not know how much I enjoy being with you. All these years we have spent many hundreds of hours together. We have played ball, gone to ball games, gone fishing, taken trips, and in general, been real buddies. Now as you grow older, I dread the day when you will not be with me; but I am grateful that we have four more years, at least, together. To be with you is always a joy and always fun. I cut up with you a lot, of course, but that is because you are my buddy, my pal, my son.

4. I am proud of you because you are willing to express your love. A lot of boys your age would think it "sissy" to be loving, but that is not true. I love you, and as you said, you love me; and we should let each other know about it. I am glad that you take time to let me know that you love me.

5. I have a lot of dreams wrapped up in you, son. I would not tell you to be a preacher. I would not tell you what to be. I would simply tell you to be clean, to be honest, and to stay in the will of God. If you do those three things, I will be the proudest dad in the world.

If I had my choice to pick any boy in the world as my son, I would pick you again. You are all that I have dreamed my boy would be. May God help you to always be that.

Now in closing, may I say this: You will have many decisions to make in the next few years. There are many questions, perhaps, that you would like to ask concerning life, etc., and I want you to feel free to come to me and say, "Hey, Dad, can I talk with you?" We will make an appointment, and you may talk about anything in the world. I want it to always be that way, just as it has been in the past.

God bless you, son. I always wanted to be a dad, and I always wanted to have a boy. I am proud of you.

Sincerely,
Dad

JH:es

It is tragic how many children feel that they cannot talk to their parents. How vital it is to keep the line of communication open.

6. *The parents should certainly share the high hours with the child.* Things that do not seem too big to us are very big to young people and children. One need only to think back to his youth and remember for a while. Then he will understand the bigness of the decisions and the events of youth. The following is a letter that I wrote to my daughter Becky as she entered high school. It was a very important letter as far as the father-daughter relationship was concerned.

September 8, 1966

Miss Becky Hyles
8232 Greenwood
Munster, Indiana

Dear Becky:

As you enter high school, I want you to know a few things and remember others. First, I want you to know what a wonderful day it was in the lives of your mother and me when we heard you were coming. You brought a new dimension to our lives. You are our oldest and will always hold a special place in our hearts.

We began praying for you nearly seven months before you were born. Thousands of days have passed since then, but we have not stopped praying for you daily. Naturally I am proud that you are in high school; but I am prouder that you are a fine, Christian girl. To be sure, there have been times we have had to scold you and even discipline you, but all of these experiences have been used to make better people out of all of us. I trust God will use them to bring about His will in your life.

Now you are going to high school, Becky. You carry with you many hopes and dreams from your mother and me. We hope you have a wonderful life in high school, and we know that you will come out of high school and go into college the same fine, clean, dedicated Christian that you are now. In order to make this possible, let me make a few suggestions:

1. Always be courteous to the teachers, but remember that no person is perfect. Do not talk back to the teachers nor express your views when they are in opposition unless the teachers ask for your views. Even then, do it in a kind, sweet, Christian way. Remember, your father has taken the courses they have taken. I have been to college, I have been to seminary, I have my doctor's degree, I have been president of a college, and I have preached in many colleges and seminaries across America. You will not have a teacher who knows more about general education than your father. I am simply saying, if you have any question concerning any subject, please ask me. If they bring up something that is contrary to the Bible that you want explained, please ask me. Also remember this: Most of the great universities in the world (even though they do not believe the Bible now) were founded by Bible-believing people. This is true in the case of Harvard, Yale, Princeton, etc.

2. Even though you are in high school every day, be sure that your best friends are Christian friends at First Baptist. This is one thing that I am proud of you for. In junior high and elementary school you kept your best friends your church friends. This is so wise. Do not even consider a date with an unsaved boy or a boy who is not dedicated. I pray that God will always let you go with boys from our own church or churches of like faith.

3. I trust that you will always trust your dad and mom and our advice and counsel. We want what is best for you and never try to advise you selfishly or for our own good. There may be times when you think our judgment is not best. If you will trust us, later on you will understand.

4. As I have said before, Becky, I think you have been privileged to have been placed in a preacher's home. To be sure, there are many inconveniences, but I think the advantages far outweigh the disadvantages. Our rules may be a little stricter than even those of your Christian friends at church, but remember that the rules by which your mother and I live are also stricter than the rules by which the other parents live. There are many things that we, as pastor and wife, cannot

enjoy, but it is worth it. I hope you will look at it this way as a pastor's daughter. You have been very sweet in accepting the rules thus far. One day we will all look back upon them and rejoice because of them.

Becky, you were a real delight during our vacation. I enjoyed being with you. Your mother enjoyed it tremendously and told me that she never saw you any more cheerful or any more the life of the party. I hope that you will always be that way. Remember, "A merry heart doeth good like a medicine." God has endowed you with a wonderful personality, and I am grateful for that.

I have prayed for you a great deal during the time you and Kenny were breaking up and the days following, and I know a little bit how heavy your heart has been. I think you have been a real trooper through it all, and I am proud of you. I am praying for you that God will have His way concerning the boys you should go with and other important decisions and phases of your life.

I just wanted to write this little note since you are going to high school and remind you again as you go to high school that you carry with you fifteen years of your parents' love, dreams, hopes, work, and in some small way, maybe even sacrifice. I would rather die than for you not to be all that God wants you to be. We will do our part to see to it that you become what He would have you to be, and I know you will do yours.

You have only four years with us here at home. Let's make them the best. I love you.

Sincerely,
Dad

JH:es

7. *The parents should always realize the bigness of the decisions that the children have to make.* My boy David is a good athlete. He wanted to go out for basketball in school. Now, I did not care if he played basketball, but I had some preference that he not. He is going to be a preacher, and I wanted him to center his life around his church and not his school. The decision was a big one for him, and consequently, a big one for me. Below is the letter that was written to Dave concerning this decision.

November 3, 1966

David Hyles
8232 Greenwood
Munster, Indiana

Dear Dave:

I know it is a big thing in your life to have the opportunity to go out for basketball. It is also a big thing in my life for you to make the right decision. When I was your age, I dreamed of having a son, which means that I have looked forward to having you for twenty-eight years or more. I always dreamed of what my son would be like. You have been that and more. At least five times in the last week people have approached me telling w h a t   a   fine boy you are and what a gentleman you are. Of course, this makes me proud.

I could not have asked for a finer son. My only request is that you continue to be what you have been. People all across America know you and have confidence in you. Many of my preacher brethren have told me they hoped their sons turn out to be what you are. The other day while in Wichita, Kansas, Brother Bill Harvey told me that you were one of the finest boys he has ever met.

Now I am sure you understand that any advice I give you would be because I love you and because I want your reputation to always be the same as it is now, so let me repeat what I told you briefly this morning: I would prefer that you not play on the school ball teams, but I will leave the decision up to you.

I naturally want you to run with the best of boys. These, of course, are to be found at church. However, I do not doubt for a minute that if you would play ball at school, you would still be a fine boy. I trust you completely. However, I would prefer that your companions always be the very best.

Do you remember last night when I was teaching you and the other boys in front of the teachers and officers? I mentioned there are some good things that are wrong to do. This does not mean that you will be sinning if you play basketball. It does

mean that you will be sinning if you do anything that is not in
God's will.

You make the decision, Dave, and I know it is a big one.
Mother and the girls could not understand how big it is, but I
know. If you decide to play basketball, I will be proud of you,
and I will lead the cheering section. If you decide not to play, I
will be equally as proud of you and will lead the cheering
section. You will not be disobeying me if you choose to play;
but again, I say, I have some preference that you don't play.

If you decide not to play, I will find a hundred ways to make
it up to you. Now you pray about it and do what you think the
Lord wants you to do. You are a good Christian and the Lord
will lead you, I am sure.

Sincerely,
Dad

JH:es

He gladly and happily made his decision not to play
basketball. As I dictate this chapter, he and I are at the Bill Rice
Ranch in Murfreesboro, Tennessee, together. He flew down
with me yesterday. We have been real buddies in every way, and
I think he is glad for his decision. This is not to say that it is
wrong for a boy to play basketball. It is to say that it is right for
parents to be vitally concerned about decisions their children
have to make.

8. *Boys should be led to become masculine, and girls should
be led to become feminine.* Dads should see to it that boys
become real boys, and moms should see to it that girls become
real girls. When David was five years of age, I got a baseball
glove, a bat, and a baseball. I hit him some grounders nearly too
hard for him to catch. I told him that I would give him a nickel
for each one he caught. The ball hit him in the chin, on the arm,
on the thumb, and most every place except the glove. He didn't
make any money but he was becoming a man. He was beginning
to take the knocks of life. I then got some boxing gloves and
had a kid a little older than David come over and box with him.
The boy was just enough better at boxing than Dave to beat
him a little bit. He knew what it was to get hit in the nose and to
be whipped. He was still becoming a man! I have worked hard

to teach him proper coordination of his body and to lead him to become a man. It has been worth it a thousand times. Dads, see to it your boys do not become sissies. Moms, see to it that your girls become ladies with all of the charm, poise, and grace that accompanies being lady-like.

This chapter is in no way an attempt to teach child rearing. It is simply a few of the meditations of a father who lies on his back at the Bill Rice Ranch late on a summer evening and who is proud of his son.

Chapter Forty-Seven

CHRISTMAS IS OVER

The Christmas season is now over. The holidays from school have ended. We are sitting around the table for breakfast on the day the children are returning to school. I look over and see tears swelling in the eyes of my youngest daughter.

"What is wrong, sweetheart?" I asked.

"I don't want to go back to school." She replies.

Then I remember how I felt on the same day of the year. I felt the same way at bedtime on Christmas night and in the closing moments of my birthday.

What causes such a feeling in the life of a child, or for that matter, in the life of an adult? Who among us has not felt the loneliness and melancholy of hating to see a delightful experience end? End they must, as all delightful experiences must in this life.

Because of this it is best that we understand our emotions at such occasions.

Why this sad feeling? Something has died. Death is an absence of life, and with the passing of each day another day has died. It will never come again. The thrill of going to bed Christmas Eve night, the beauty of the tree Christmas morning, the opening of the presents, the playing with the toys, the delicious and beautiful Christmas dinner have now joined all of the other days and experiences of the past. These particular ones will never come again.

Of course, the sadness comes from looking back. Yesterday is always dead; tomorrow is alive. Looking backward may bring sadness, but looking forward will bring gladness. *One of the secrets of the Christian life is looking forward to tomorrow. Remember that on the day before yesterday, yesterday was tomorrow, and yesterday, today was tomorrow. As long as there is a tomorrow with its hopes, there can be a happy today.*

How can my child (and her father) overcome such a feeling of melancholy?

1. Learn the art of enjoying today. It is wonderful to look forward to tomorrow; it is more wonderful to enjoy tomorrow on the morrow. *One must work hard in filling yesterday's expectations for today. In so doing, not only does it enhance the joy of today and increase the joy of yesterday, but it brightens the prospects for joy tomorrow. Far too many of us have never known to enjoy today up to yesterday's predictions.* In other words, let us be happy while having happiness. It is not enough to look forward to the happiness we are going to have tomorrow nor to look backward to the happiness we had yesterday. We must recognize the happiness we are having today. Most of us look forward to having friends before we get them, weep because of their loss after we have had them, but fail to enjoy their friendship while we have them. How many ladies look forward twenty years to becoming a mother and look backward for forty years or more to having been active in fulfilling the duties of a mother and yet complained during the twenty years in which they were that for which they had looked forward and now to which they look backward. Let us be careful to let the day fulfill the expectations of yesterday, and our enjoyment of today will be as much today as it will be in tomorrow's memories.

2. Plan joy in giving and not receiving. If one's Christmas is receiving, he can only have Christmas when someone decides to give to him. If one's Christmas is in giving, then every day can be a Christmas for him. Our wills cannot determine how much we receive nor how often we can receive. They can, however, determine how often we can give. *If Christmas to us is unwrapping, then it can only come periodically. If it is wrapping, it can come daily.* Let us look forward to being the giver and not the receiver. Then on the evening of Christmas we can still look forward to Christmas tomorrow and tomorrow and tomorrow.

3. Raise the floor of our lives and not the roof. One's happiness depends not on the height of his heights but the height of his depths. How high are you on your lowest day? How high you are on your lowest day determines your happiness, not how high you are on your highest day. How happy are you on March 24? July 18? October 3? When your lowest days become happier days, then the step down from Christmas will not be such a big one. Hence, let us not stress so much the raising of the roof as the raising of the floor.

Chapter Forty-Eight

THE GLORY OF YOUR ABSENCE

Your presence yesterday was sweet, and the hope of seeing you tomorrow is blessed; yet today I have stumbled across a rare jewel that I named, THE GLORY OF YOUR ABSENCE. I had not planned for it, and I died when you left yesterday and had not planned a resurrection until I see you tomorrow. Yet rise I did in the energy of THE GLORY OF YOUR ABSENCE.

In your absence I have measured you. This I could not do properly yesterday, for I was with you. Now, in THE GLORY OF YOUR ABSENCE, I measure you without the persuasion of your beauty and find you are today exactly what I thought you were yesterday and what I dream you will be tomorrow.

In THE GLORY OF YOUR ABSENCE I can see you with the soul and not be hampered by our "glass darkly's."

In THE GLORY OF YOUR ABSENCE my love is proven to you in a new way, for now it is only your soul that makes captive my attention.

It is during the GLORY OF YOUR ABSENCE when I pledge to never again take for granted your presence. Only then can I properly savor the times of your presence yesterday and prepare for your presence tomorrow, that I may learn to adequately appreciate tomorrow's fellowship.

So THE GLORY OF YOUR ABSENCE is really THE GLORY OF YOUR PRESENCE, for in a mysterious way we are knitted. Hence, absence is impossible, for we are always present, for to be absent from the body is to be present with the soul.

Oh, I still prefer the blessing of your presence and will leap at your footsteps tomorrow, but today our souls shall walk together in THE GLORY OF YOUR ABSENCE.

Chapter Forty-Nine

STRENGTH AND BEAUTY

"It is not easy to lose, but often more is won in loss than in victory."

"Great victories in the future are often won by graceful losses in the past."

"A request from a friend is a royal command."

"A tear today is an investment in a laugh tomorrow."

"Gentleness is love wrapped in character."

"Silence says what the silent man is."

"To please a friend is a welcome bonus; to help him is the great reward."

"Greatness is always wrapped in simplicity."

"Even if a task is not worthy of you, diligence is!"

"Being loved is life's second greatest blessing; loving is the greatest."

"Even if the task you do is not big, the way you do it can be big."

"Faith is doing everything I can do and trusting God to do what I cannot do. God can do what I cannot do, but He will not do what I can do if I refuse to do it!"

"Our difference is caused by the sum total of our differences."

"It is easy to be grateful for a bonus; it is character to be grateful for a salary."

"The more you appreciate the little the more you will enjoy the average."

"If I live for self, I can live only for one; if I live for others, I can live for 3,000,000,000."

"If you take away the God of the morals, you no longer have the morals of God."

"There is no life as 'empty' as the 'self-centered' life; there is no life as 'centered' as the 'self-emptied' life."

"If you have won the right to know how it feels to lose, your entire ministry will be wrapped up in making winners out of losers."

"Make no provision for failure."

"Life is like a game. To lose the first down does not mean loss of the game. To be behind at the end of the first quarter does not mean the game will be lost."

"Character is the subconscious doing of right."

"Personality will grow old, but character does not."

"The *existence* of love is because of character; the *degree* of the love is because of the object of this love."

"It is better to be *too* blunt than *two*-faced!"

"Personality without wisdom is 'a character.' "

"Don't ever tell all you know on any subject; someone may ask you a question when you're through."

"A person who will not take care of little things will not take care of big things, for big things are but an accumulation of little things."

"Use your work to build your people, not your people to build your work."

"If you'll work at doing the things you *ought* to do, the Lord will help you NOT do the things you *ought not* do."

"You are not dependent upon people *thinking* you are humble as long as God *knows* you are."

"I'd rather be a *free* man in slavery than to be *enslaved* to a group which will offer me freedom."

"Every man knows something I do not know. I must probe until I find it; hence, all men are my teachers."

"I'd rather be a good Christian than a good preacher."

"I'd rather do right wrongly than wrong rightly."

"The time spent between the opportunity to do right and the doing of right is time spent justifying the doing of wrong."

"Once you've tasted the heavenly manna of forgiveness you'll never want to eat from the Devil's garbage can of vindicativeness again."

"I'd rather conserve two (converts) out of 100 than one out of one."

"It's good to obtain knowledge through study; it is better to obtain both knowledge and character through study and obedience."

"The only lasting thing you can ever get for yourself comes from the leftovers when you give to others."

"Forced gentleness is weakness."

"Love is hate turned inside out."

"Contrast is essential for a quality to exist."

"There's no way to have any virtue unless you have the potential for its opposite."

"He who knows no tempest knows no calm."

"Goodness that comes without temptation is not true goodness, for it is based on necessity, not conviction."

"Forced humility is inferiority."

"Without a potential for temper, gentleness is mere cowardice."

"You're not a good Christian because you reach heights, but you're a good Christian because you don't reach depths."